EVERYDAY CELEBRATIONS

everyday celebrations

savoring FOOD, FAMILY, and LIFE at home

by donata maggipinto

photographs by france ruffenach

CHRONICLE BOOKS

SAN FRANCISCO

Library of Congress Cataloging-
in-Publication Data:
Maggipinto, Donata.
Everyday celebrations : savoring
food, family, and life at home /
Donata Maggipinto; photographs
by France Ruffenach. p. cm.
ISBN 0-8118-4487-0

1. Cookery, American.
2. Handicraft.
3. Entertaining.
4. Menus.
I. Title.
TX715.M2116 2005
642'.4—dc22

2004025643

Manufactured in China.

Designed by Lesley Feldman
Prop styling by Aaron Hom
Assistant prop styling by
    Elizabeth Glass, Scott Amiss
Food styling by Pouke
Assistant food styling by
    Jeff Larsen

The photographer wishes
to thank Donata Maggipinto
for inspirational content,
Jeff and Amanda Marcus for
allowing access to their
beautiful home, Aaron Hom
for his perfect sense of style,
Pouke for gorgeous food,
Sara Schneider for her guid-
ance, and the following vendors
for their generosity:

Dandelion
55 Potrero Avenue
San Francisco, California 94103
415-436-9500

Ellington & French
2942 Domingo Avenue
Berkeley, California 94705
510-548-8188

The Gardener
1836 Fourth Street
Berkeley, California 94710
510-548-4545

Distributed in Canada
by Raincoast Books
9050 Shaughnessy Street
Vancouver, British Columbia
V6P 6E5

10 9 8 7 6 5 4 3 2 1

Chronicle Books LLC
85 Second Street
San Francisco, California 94105
www.chroniclebooks.com

Gentle Reminder: Never
leave an open flame unattended,
be it candle or fireplace.

FOR COURTNEY, REYN,
AND CHANCE

And in memory of Saba and Feather, who cheerfully
ate the crumbs when I cooked and patiently sat at my feet as I wrote.
For thirteen and fifteen years respectively, these dogs
were this gal's best friends.

CONTENTS

INTRODUCTION

Celebrate Every Day · page 8

Chapter *No.* One
SPRING SENSATIONS

Spring Celebrations · page 12
Garden-Inspired Lunch · page 25
Easy Asian Kitchen Party · page 39

Chapter *No.* Three
AUTUMN SENSATIONS

Autumn Celebrations · page 94
Soup for Supper · page 107
Autumn Birthday Celebration · page 123

Chapter *No.* Two
SUMMER SENSATIONS

Summer Celebrations · page 54
Red. White. and Blueberry Breakfast · page 65
Paella Party · page 77

Chapter *No.* Four
WINTER SENSATIONS

Winter Celebrations · page 138
Charades and Chardonnay · page 151
Sunday Dinner · page 165

ACKNOWLEDGMENTS · *page 176*
INDEX · *page 177*
TABLE OF EQUIVALENTS · *page 180*

Home, sensational home. Filled with love and laughter,
family and friends, food for the body and beauty for the soul, home
is our sensory touchstone.

Our five senses can bring us immeasurable pleasure. The sight of the first crocus peeking through the snow. The song of swallows in the early evening. The whisper-softness of vintage linen on our fingers. The aroma of quince piled in a bowl on the hall table. The taste of a just-picked strawberry or tomato.

I've added another sense to this list: awareness and appreciation and love for our family, friends, and the natural world that surrounds us.

There ought to be a moment in every day when the world stops and we pause to reengage with our senses, and reconnect with those we love and the gifts that nature bestows on us. Family, friends, food, and beautiful flourishes are life's graces, and we ought to celebrate them every day. *Everyday Celebrations* will inspire you to do just that.

An everyday celebration is *not* a momentous occasion requiring pomp, circumstance, and a Herculean effort. You need not study the Great Books. An everyday celebration is a wonderful moment, a temporary exit from the freeway of life, if you will. It's a casual gathering of family and friends. It's a party given for the sole pleasure of playing charades and sipping Chardonnay. It's a Sunday afternoon spent making applesauce with your children. An everyday celebration is as simple as a pleasing style note for the table or for your home: a bouquet of fall leaves or a robin's egg tucked into a nest of orange embroidery floss.

I watch my little boy, Reyn, take such delight in the smallest details that the simplest activity becomes a memorable experience. He loves to juice pink grapefruits not only for the kick he gets out of the whir of the juicer, but also because he says the grapefruits smell like sunshine. Setting the table involves browsing our linen drawers and conversing about the various colors and patterns. We can opt for coral or cornflower, polka dot or cabana stripe. Watch your children. They'll clue you in, too.

Everyday Celebrations is your guide for creating gatherings, food, and style notes for your table and home that are as delicious as they are delightful, as pretty as they are pleasurable, and as simple as they are sumptuous. My intention is to inspire you by giving you examples of my everyday celebrations so you can express your creative self in the ways that mean the most to you — and have fun doing it.

In the pages that follow are eight everyday celebrations, complete with style ideas and menus that incorporate quick, prepurchased treats. The recipes are simple and time-efficient, with an emphasis on fresh, seasonal ingredients. The decorating ideas are both imaginative and doable. No degree in arts and crafts is required! From a Red, White, and Blueberry Breakfast and an Easy Asian Kitchen Party to recipes for rhubarb chutney, berry syllabub (What is that, you ask? See page 57), and root beer floats, you will discover plenty of ways to engage your senses.

Seasonal celebrations set the tone for each section, with quick style ideas that bring the season into your home. You will find straightforward instructions for making May Day baskets, rosewater tonic, twine candleholders, a gourd doorstop, a persimmon and quince arrangement, and a cake-stand condiment server, among other ideas. Each season includes a "sit and sip" beverage that I hope will prompt you to do just that.

I've organized the book by season because this is the way I live my life. The seasons give the year a natural rhythm, and they give me a certain rhythm, too. When I live in accordance with what is happening outside, I am happy inside.

We share conversation and laughter with others because they nourish our souls. We share good food because it nourishes our bodies. We adorn our homes and our lives in ways that celebrate the beauty of nature and engage our senses. Thus, we create meaningful moments and enrich our days.

With *Everyday Celebrations* as your inspiration and guide, I hope you'll savor the deliciousness of each day.

spring sensations

SEARCH for robins' eggs, BREATHE IN the damp earth,
GET CAUGHT in a rain shower, SIP May wine, LISTEN to the birds,
PICK strawberries, BE a fool, GATHER pussy willows,
BAKE shortcake, SAVE an earthworm, HANG sheets in the breeze,
SHELL peas, PLANT a lilac tree, RENEW,

carry on a spring romance with your senses every temperate day.

SPRING CELEBRATIONS

Proof positive that there is a tender shoot in even the coldest ground,
March shepherds in spring lamb, daffodils, and Mother's Day.
This season of soft colors and delicate flavors reminds us that there is the
potential in each of us for beginning anew, too.

Nature has a way of drawing our senses to the outside world. In spring, after a season of muted hues, we see the emergence of true color, whether it's a patch of grass unveiled by melting snow or the flash of scarlet on a red-wing blackbird. We hear a certain buzz. I've never been sure about the source of the buzz, but scientific sorts tell me it emits from baby insects. I prefer to think that it is the sound of the natural world awakening. We feel raindrops on our head and the cheering warmth of a young sun. We touch the earth as we plant seedlings on a temperate weekend. We caress the head of a downy chick at Eastertime. We taste earthy asparagus and sweet, jewel-like strawberries.

The style ideas in this section will inspire you to wake up from winter and create a vignette with eggs, plant a violet terrarium, and make flower votives, among other ideas. The spring celebrations that follow, one an airy Garden-Inspired Lunch (page 25) and the other a come-one-come-all Easy Asian Kitchen Party (page 39), combine the season's fresh ingredients in simple yet sumptuous recipes and offer table-decorating ideas that are as bright as a spring morning.

What can you do to celebrate spring in an everyday way? Consider rhubarb. The first spring vegetable to emerge from the still-cold ground, rhubarb is a winning ingredient when paired with ginger and sugar. Its translucent pink color does not fade when cooked, giving you a dish that not only tastes delicious but looks delightful, too. Whether you're already a rhubarb enthusiast or a novice, give Rhubarb Chutney (page 19) a try. But make it soon. Fresh rhubarb is fleeting, and that makes it all the more wonderful.

When I think fleeting, I think fluttering. Wouldn't it be nice to salute spring with a bird and butterfly garden? Even if you have only a window box or a planter, you can still attract birds and butterflies. They're wonderful to watch as you sip your morning coffee. Among the flowers that are appealing to our fluttering friends are amaranths, black-eyed Susans, cosmos, delphiniums, purple coneflowers, salvias, sunflowers, trumpet vines, and zinnias. If you know a bird- or butterfly-lover, why not assemble a gift of seed packets or seedlings and bestow it on her?

"Why not?" is the operative phrase for spring. Why not give a garden lunch, whether you have a garden or not? Garden can mean a location, but it can also be a kind of décor. The Garden-Inspired Lunch features quintessential springtime foods such as asparagus and strawberries and a spring-green palette with a birdcage centerpiece. Why not host your best girlfriends, or the bridesmaids of a friend about to be wed, or a mother-to-be? The menu is just right for an Easter gathering, too. As you'll see, it's an all-purpose spring celebration theme that is fanciful and fun.

Why not try something new this spring? If a Violet Terrarium (page 20) is not your cup of tea, how about transforming tea towels into place mats or a runner (page 22)? Vintage dish or tea towels add crisp color and homeyness wherever they are placed. Don't let them languish in the kitchen drawer! Use them as place mats or stitch a few together to make a simple, attractive runner.

The Easy Asian Kitchen Party includes familiar foods enlivened with Asian flavors, among them roast chicken marinated with soy sauce, hoisin sauce, ginger, lime, and mint, and green beans stir-fried with Chinese rice wine, sesame oil, and smoked sausage. Then there's Tropical Fruits Foster (page 51), an exotic riff on the old-fashioned banana dessert. Yum! With easy-to-find ingredients and vibrant recipes that lend themselves to many hands in the kitchen, this Asian menu is perfect to welcome spring. In fact, wouldn't it be fun to celebrate April Fool's Day in an Asian way?

When you experience the season with your senses, spring's offerings reveal themselves in delightful ways. I love the first spring day that I walk through the farmers' market and encounter the farmer with his paper lunch bags overflowing with English peas. If you have the pleasure of shelling peas, a methodical act that, by its very nature, causes you to slow down, you won't be able to stop yourself from eating one, two, three, or thirty of the sweet, velvety raw orbs. If any peas remain after shelling, steam them and toss them with sweet butter and mint. Heaven.

Experience the egg, Easter's icon, in new ways. Contact a nearby farm and ask if you can gather eggs from the henhouse. I did this at the Ballymaloe Cooking School in Ireland years ago, and the memory of it returns to me every Easter: the hen's pride (I swear it), the warmth of the egg under her, the elegance of its simplicity. Immerse eggs in colorful dyes and hang them from pussy willow branches. Remove the tops of eggs, wash the eggs, add a bit of water, and insert small posies such as pansies or crocuses. And don't wait for the weekend to make an egg breakfast. Turn a weekday morning into an everyday celebration by making scrambled eggs mixed with an array of fresh herbs (perhaps plucked from your windowsill herb garden).

Some say January is the month for resolving to do something new. I say it's spring. Why else would a season be synonymous with leaping, launching, and jumping off? Happy landing!

Project *No.* One

CRYSTALLIZED FLOWERS

Spring's first flowers — violets, Johnny-jump-ups, and pansies among them — are edible and just the right size for crystallizing into small sugared jewels for decorating cakes and cookies. Stir a pinch of salt into 1 or 2 egg whites and whisk to blend. Using a small paintbrush, carefully paint the flowers with the egg white. Dip into superfine sugar, place on waxed paper, and sprinkle with more sugar. Transfer to a wire rack to dry for 2 to 3 days. Store in an airtight container for up to 1 month.

Project *No.* Two

ELEGANT EGGS

Don't relegate eggs to Easter morning. Use these graceful ovoids to create a springtime vignette on a hall table or sideboard. Fill small galvanized pails or grass baskets with bird seed, and nestle blown-out eggs, natural or colored, in them. For an unusual and eye-catching tableau, rest one or two blue robins' eggs in a homemade nest of bright orange embroidery floss.

Project *No.* Three

CUPCAKE GREETINGS

Arrange cupcakes on a platter and decorate the tops with letters piped with icing or cut from purchased refrigerated sugar-cookie dough. Allot one letter to each cupcake and spell "Happy Birthday" or "Best Wishes" or somebody's name. It's a fun and delicious dessert.

Project *No.* Four

BIRD IN THE GRASS CENTERPIECE

Here's an activity for the kids: Send them outdoors to collect the longest, greenest blades of grass they can find. When they return, gather the grass, trim the ends evenly with scissors, and place in a footed glass container filled with about 1 inch of water. If you wish, anchor the grass with dried split peas (rinsed well!) or marbles. Perch a bird ornament on the edge of the container, or arrange millinery butterflies in and around the centerpiece.

Project *No.* Five

MAY DAY (OR ANY DAY) BASKETS

The charming custom of anonymously leaving flower-filled May Day baskets on doorknobs dates from the Middle Ages. Make May Day "baskets" from glass jars, metal cans, or cardboard. For a sweet salute to the season, use an empty can of peas (the Le Seur – brand label is beautiful!). Punch 2 holes, opposite each other, about ½ inch from the top edge. Thread ribbon through the holes and knot it at each end to create a handle. Fill with water and flowers. Hang on a neighbor's door.

Project *No.* Six

CAKE-STAND CONDIMENT SERVER

Transform a pedestal cake stand into a tabletop condiment server. Arrange salt, pepper, mustard, soy sauce, Tabasco, and other frequently used condiments on the stand for easy transport to the table and attractive service while you're dining. Store on a kitchen counter or sideboard when not in use.

Project *No.* Seven

RHUBARB CHUTNEY

Rhubarb is one of spring's first flavors. Paired with fresh ginger, raisins, and the subtle essence of lime, it makes tart-sweet chutney. Serve this with chicken or pork.

makes about two cups

¼ cup balsamic vinegar · ½ cup red wine vinegar
½ cup sugar · ⅛ teaspoon ground cloves · 1 teaspoon grated lime zest
½ cup golden raisins · ¼ cup peeled and sliced fresh ginger
1¼ pounds rhubarb cut into 1-inch pieces (remove any leaves,
as they are toxic) · ½ cup boiling water

In a saucepan, combine the vinegars, sugar, cloves, lime zest, raisins, and ginger. Bring to a boil over medium-high heat, then reduce the heat to medium-low and simmer, uncovered, until the raisins soften, about 5 minutes. Add the rhubarb and the boiling water. Continue to cook, stirring occasionally, until the rhubarb is soft, about 20 minutes. If any liquid remains, cook over high heat until it almost evaporates. Transfer the chutney to a bowl and let cool. Chutney will keep, covered, for up to 2 weeks.

Project *No.* Eight

FRESH FLOWER VOTIVES

In addition to offering their beauty and scent to a table, large flower blossoms, such as roses and peonies, can serve as votive candleholders, too. Cut the stem so the flower lies flat, or nest it in a shallow bowl. Hollow out a portion of the bloom's center and nestle a tea light or votive candle in it.

Project *No.* Nine

VIOLET TERRARIUM

Everybody remembers the third-grade terrarium project. It's time to put those skills to use as an adult, perhaps with a child in tow. Liberate the violet from its "shrinking" reputation and create a stunning terrarium that mimics this flower's woodland environment.

Select a clear glass container such as a fishbowl. Put in a 1-inch layer of fishbowl gravel, then 1 to 2 inches of activated charcoal (available at pet stores). Fill the container about one-third full with bark-based potting soil. Gently lower 1 or 2 violet plants into the terrarium. Add a bit more potting soil, using it to anchor the plants. Cover the soil with moistened sphagnum moss. Add distilled water (tap water has chemicals that will inhibit the plants' growth). Cover the terrarium with a tight-fitting lid (a plate or pot lid, for example) or plastic wrap. After a few days, if you notice condensation on the inside of the container, there is too much moisture inside. Remove the lid for a day or so to allow the moisture to evaporate, then replace the lid. Place in a shady window for all to enjoy.

Project *No.* Ten

SIT AND SIP: LIMONCELLO

This Italian *digestivo* looks and tastes like sunlight. Though enjoyed throughout Italy, it is relatively unknown here. That's too bad, as it is quite delightful. One sip and I think you will become a proponent, too. If you make Limoncello in March, it will be ready for Easter and Mother's Day celebrations.

makes about six cups
Zest stripped from 2 pounds scrubbed lemons
4 cups unflavored vodka · 3 cups sugar · 3 cups water

Put the lemon zest in a large bowl and pour the vodka over it. Cover the bowl and let stand for 1 week at room temperature.

In a large saucepan, combine the sugar and water and cook over medium heat, stirring, until the sugar dissolves. Remove from the heat and let cool to warm. Add to the vodka mixture and stir well. Strain the liquid into sterilized bottles; seal and refrigerate for at least 1 month or up to 1 year.

Serve very cold, in small glasses.

Project *No.* Eleven

TEA TOWEL PLACE MATS AND RUNNER

Bring your vintage dish or tea towels out into the light of day. Employ them as place mats or stitch some together to make a table runner.

GARDEN-INSPIRED LUNCH

MENU

Cherry Tomato, Arugula, *and* Prosciutto Salad

Asparagus *and* Basil Frittata

Chicken Croquettes *with* Buttermilk-Herb Dressing

Strawberries *with* Chilled Zabaglione

You don't have to be a gardener to appreciate the pleasures of the garden.
The harmonious palette of blossoms and leaves, the interplay of light and shadows,
and the fragrances —the fragrances!—send the senses into rapture.

I particularly like the garden in springtime when everything is new and intensely aromatic, as if the flowers are expressing the joy of awakening in the sun after a long winter.

This lunch is a celebration of the garden and a gentle reminder that nature is all around us every day, just waiting for us to reap pleasure and rejuvenation from its gifts. Whether your garden is a full-blown English medley of roses, delphiniums, and hydrangeas; pots of herbs on a windowsill; a pitcher of daisies; or a picture book that you leaf through on spring's soft evenings, celebrate it every day!

I have hosted garden lunches like this one for various occasions, including a baby shower, engagement party, and a best-friends get-together. While the lunch need not take place outdoors, it's fun to transform the table into a garden. I chose a spring-green palette for this lunch, including a vintage 1950s floral tablecloth. I pressed ferns and tiny spring flowers between white plates and glass plates so that everybody could sit down to their personal garden. A 1940s green birdcage became the centerpiece, filled with moss and a vase of white flowers, including lilies of the valley, hydrangeas, and spray roses. The birdcage is trimmed with trailing ivy, and millinery birds are wired to the top.

A menu I enjoyed in Italy a few springs ago inspired this one. As pretty as it is light, it includes a lovely Cherry Tomato, Arugula, and Prosciutto Salad; a satisfying frittata that can be served warm or at room temperature; chicken-and-herb croquettes, drizzled with a tangy dressing; and, for dessert, strawberries with zabaglione, an ethereal Italian custard.

Cherry Tomato, Arugula, *and* Prosciutto Salad

SERVES SIX AS PART OF A LUNCH BUFFET

A celebration of robust flavors, this salad is best assembled
at the last minute, though the ingredients may be prepared beforehand.
Ricotta salata, a smooth, firm sheep's milk cheese from Italy that is similar
to feta, tops the salad. Its mild, salty flavor complements
the salad beautifully.

In a medium bowl, combine the halved tomatoes with the garlic, basil,
1 tablespoon of the olive oil, and the salt and pepper. Using the back of a
large spoon, gently press the tomatoes to release some of their juices.
Divide the tomato mixture among 6 plates and arrange the arugula, radicchio, prosciutto and shaved cheese on top. Drizzle with the vinegar and
remaining 2 tablespoons olive oil. Season with a bit more salt and pepper
to taste.

List *of* Ingredients

16 cherry tomatoes, halved · 2 garlic cloves , thinly sliced · 1 cup fresh basil leaves, thinly sliced ·
3 tablespoons extra-virgin olive oil · Salt and freshly ground pepper to taste ·
3 cups arugula leaves · 6 to 8 radicchio leaves, torn into bite-sized pieces · 4 ounces thinly sliced
prosciutto, shredded · 4 ounces ricotta salata or Parmesan cheese, shaved ·
1 tablespoon balsamic vinegar

Asparagus *and* Basil Frittata

SERVES SIX AS PART OF A LUNCH BUFFET

Frittata, a sturdy Italian omelet, wonderfully showcases
seasonal vegetables and herbs. In this case, asparagus and basil come
together in a harmonious flavor marriage.

Preheat the broiler. In a large bowl, beat the eggs, milk, cheese, salt, and pepper together until just blended. In a small bowl, combine the herbs and lemon zest; set aside.

In a 12-inch ovenproof skillet (or 2 smaller skillets), melt the butter with the olive oil over medium-high heat. When the butter foams, add the onion and cook until soft, about 3 minutes. Add the asparagus, spreading evenly to cover the bottom of the skillet. Pour the eggs over the asparagus, reduce the heat to low, and cook until the eggs are just firm around the edges, 4 to 5 minutes. Using a spatula, lift the edges and tilt the pan to let the uncooked eggs run underneath. Cook 2 minutes more, then sprinkle the top with half the herb mixture and place under the broiler. Cook until the top is set and golden brown, 3 to 4 minutes.

Remove the skillet from the oven and run a knife around the edges of the frittata. Invert a plate on top of the skillet, and holding the plate and the skillet together firmly (with potholders!), turn them over, releasing the frittata onto the plate. Sprinkle with the remaining herb mixture. Cut into wedges and serve warm or at room temperature.

List *of* Ingredients

8 eggs • 3 tablespoons whole milk • 1/3 cup grated Parmesan cheese • 1 teaspoon salt •
½ teaspoon freshly ground pepper • 1/3 cup chopped fresh basil • 2 tablespoons chopped fresh flat-leaf (Italian) parsley •
1 tablespoon grated lemon zest • 2 tablespoons unsalted butter • 1 tablespoon
extra-virgin olive oil • ½ yellow onion, finely chopped • 12 asparagus spears, trimmed
and cut into 1-inch pieces (about 3 cups)

Chicken Croquettes
with Buttermilk-Herb Dressing

SERVES SIX AS PART OF A LUNCH BUFFET

Minced chicken croquettes with a crisp crust, dressed with
a tangy buttermilk-herb dressing, spell "delightful." It's a dish that is at once
delicate and satisfying—just right for a spring lunch.

In a large sauté pan, add the bouquet garni to the chicken broth and bring to a boil. Add the chicken breasts, reduce the heat to low, and simmer, turning once or twice, until opaque throughout, about 15 minutes.

Transfer the chicken breasts to a plate and let cool to the touch. Discard the bouquet garni and save the broth for another use. Pat the chicken breasts dry with paper towels and coarsely chop them. In a food processor, combine the chicken, bread, parsley, eggs, salt, and pepper. Process until slightly coarse. Using a bit of flour to coat your hands, form the chicken mixture into 12 oval croquettes.

In a large sauté pan, heat the olive oil over medium-high heat. Add the chicken croquettes in batches (do not crowd them or they will not brown nicely), and cook until golden brown, turning once, about 3 to 5 minutes. Transfer to paper towels to drain, and keep warm in a 250°F oven while cooking the rest. Add more oil if necessary to coat the pan between batches.

Serve warm, with the dressing alongside.

List *of* Ingredients

Bouquet garni: 1 bay leaf, 2 sprigs thyme, and 2 sprigs parsley tied with kitchen twine •
3 cups chicken broth • 3 boneless, skinless chicken breast halves • 2 slices stale white bread, crust removed,
soaked in milk for 10 minutes and squeezed dry • $\frac{1}{3}$ cup minced fresh flat-leaf parsley •
3 eggs, beaten lightly • 1 teaspoon salt • ½ teaspoon freshly ground pepper • ¼ cup olive oil •
Buttermilk-Herb Dressing (page 34)

Buttermilk-Herb Dressing

MAKES ABOUT TWO CUPS

It's hard to believe, but this rich dressing is made with nonfat dairy ingredients. The creaminess is a nice foil for the crisp croquettes, and the piquancy adds verve.

In a food processor, combine all the ingredients. Purée until smooth. Serve immediately, or cover and refrigerate for up to 1 day.

List *of* Ingredients

6 green onions, green parts only, chopped · 2 garlic cloves, minced ·
1 cup minced fresh flat-leaf (Italian) parsley · 1 bunch watercress, trimmed and finely chopped ·
½ cup nonfat buttermilk · ½ cup low-fat sour cream · 2 tablespoons mayonnaise ·
Juice of 1 lemon · 1 teaspoon salt · ¼ teaspoon freshly ground pepper

Strawberries
with Chilled Zabaglione

SERVES SIX AS A DESSERT

Unlike the traditional version of zabaglione that is served warm,
my rendition is whisked over ice until cool. This way, you can make the zabaglione
2 to 3 hours ahead of time and refrigerate it. Then, all you have to do is
spoon it over the strawberries when it's time for dessert. For an extra-special
presentation, make the crystallized flowers and use them
to garnish this dessert. Pretty!

In a large bowl, combine the strawberries, ¼ cup of the wine, and the
5 tablespoons sugar. Cover and refrigerate until chilled, about 1 hour,
tossing carefully once or twice.

Fill a large bowl with ice cubes and add a little water; set aside.

Bring a saucepan with 2 inches of water to a gentle simmer. Put the egg
yolks in a stainless-steel bowl. Using a balloon whisk or handheld electric
mixer, beat the egg yolks with the remaining ⅓ cup sugar until light and
frothy. Add the remaining ¾ cup wine and whisk until well blended. Place
the bowl over the pan of simmering water; do not allow the bottom of the
bowl to touch the water. Whisk constantly, scraping the bottom and sides

recipe continues on page 37 »

Strawberries *with* Chilled Zabaglione

continued

of the bowl, until the mixture has tripled in volume and begins to hold soft peaks, 10 to 15 minutes. Watch the mixture carefully! If it gets too hot, it will curdle.

Transfer the bowl from the pan to the bowl of ice, nesting it securely. Continue to whisk until the mixture is room temperature, scraping the bottom and sides often, 8 to 10 minutes. The mixture will be very thick.

In a deep bowl, whip the cream until stiff peaks form. Stir in the lemon zest. Using a rubber spatula, gently fold the whipped cream into the egg mixture until thoroughly combined. Serve immediately, or cover and refrigerate for 2 to 3 hours; whisk gently before serving.

Spoon the berries into bowls and top generously with the zabaglione. Garnish with mint leaves and crystallized flowers, if using.

List *of* Ingredients

8 cups ripe strawberries, halved lengthwise • 1 cup sweet Marsala wine •
5 tablespoons sugar, plus ⅓ cup • 4 egg yolks • ¾ cup heavy cream • 1½ teaspoons grated lemon zest •
Fresh mint leaves and/or crystallized flowers (page 14) for garnish (optional)

EASY ASIAN KITCHEN PARTY

MENU

Potstickers *and* Egg Rolls

Salt *and* Pepper Shrimp

Roast Chicken *with* Asian Flavors

Refreshing Cucumber Salad

Coconut Rice

Smoky Green Beans

Tropical Fruits Foster

Fortune Cookies

I'm fortunate to live near a thriving Chinatown where the markets
and restaurants offer exotic and delicious foods. The aromas
alone are enough to entice me to walk through the neighborhood and poke
my head into the little cafés and shops that line the streets.

The cleavers chopping and the housewives yelling in the butcher shops, coupled with the elegant calligraphy of Chinese characters identifying meats, poultry, and prices, transport me to another world.

Asian food is particularly conducive to family-style eating—and cooking. Prepping the ingredients beforehand, placing them in small bowls, and creating cooking stations with the appropriate cutting and mixing equipment at the ready make it fun to cook an Asian meal together with family and friends.

The Asian recipes in this menu are just right for communal cooking. They are not complicated, nor do they include myriad ingredients, and they require different cooking methods, alleviating a bottleneck at the stove. Pass out photocopied recipes, ask for volunteers for each recipe, and discuss the menu. If someone does not want to cook, he or she can refresh drinks and pass potstickers and egg rolls purchased at a local Chinese restaurant earlier in the day.

Eat your culinary masterpieces at the kitchen table. It's a colorful menu, so provide a vivid setting. For this party, I covered the kitchen islands with Chinese newspapers. Kitchen glasses became colorful vases by slipping small paper lanterns over them. Fill the glasses with water and insert brightly colored blooms such as alliums and orchids. Don't forget to hang paper lanterns, too. For a festive touch, I attached tassels to them. Chinese takeout boxes containing tea bags, fortune cookies, and tea-scented candles were the party favors.

Salt *and* Pepper Shrimp

SERVES SIX AS A FIRST COURSE

This is not only a delicious dish but it's fun to eat, too. Each person
is given a small dish with salt, pepper, and a lime wedge. He or she squeezes the
lime onto the salt and pepper, mixes it, and then dips the shrimp into
the mixture before eating. The salty-piquant-sour flavor harmony of the "dip"
perfectly complements the smoky grilled shrimp.

Light a fire in a charcoal grill or preheat a gas grill to medium.

Rinse the shrimp in cold water. Drain and pat dry with paper towels.
Place the shrimp in a large bowl and add the lime zest, lime juice, coconut
milk, and the 1 teaspoon each of salt and pepper. Toss to coat. Let stand at
room temperature for 10 minutes.

Cut the limes into 8 wedges. Place 1 wedge in each of 6 small bowls or
dishes. Place 1 tablespoon each of sea salt and pepper in separate mounds
alongside the lime wedges in each bowl or dish.

Arrange the shrimp on the grill and cook, turning, until evenly pink,
about 1½ minutes per side.

Transfer the shrimp to a serving plate. Squeeze the juice of the remaining 2 lime wedges over the shrimp and serve immediately. To eat, squeeze
the lime wedge over the salt and pepper and stir to incorporate. Peel the
shrimp and dip it into the mixture.

List *of* Ingredients

2½ pounds jumbo shrimp in the shell · 1 tablespoon grated lime zest ·
⅓ cup fresh lime juice, plus 2 large ripe limes · ¼ cup fresh or canned coconut milk ·
1 teaspoon, plus 6 tablespoons sea salt · 1 teaspoon, plus 6 tablespoons
freshly ground white pepper

Roast Chicken *with* Asian Flavors

SERVES SIX AS A MAIN COURSE

At once sweet and spicy, this roast chicken is heady
with the flavors of Asia, among them ginger, lime, soy, and sesame. If you wish,
you can marinate the chicken the night before. If you have any left over,
use it to make Chinese chicken salad. Look for the Asian ingredients in the ethnic
foods section of your supermarket.

Combine all the ingredients except the chicken in a large bowl. Stir well.
Add the chicken pieces and coat well with the marinade. Let stand at room
temperature for 30 minutes.

Preheat the oven to 450°F. Place the chicken in a baking dish, skin side
up. Transfer the marinade to a small saucepan, bring to a boil over medium
heat, and cook for 5 minutes. Cook the chicken, basting occasionally with
the marinade, until the chicken is opaque throughout, 40 to 50 minutes.

List *of* Ingredients

¾ cup hoisin sauce • ¾ cup Chinese rice wine (Shaoxing wine) • ⅓ cup soy sauce •
2 tablespoons grated fresh ginger • 2 tablespoons fresh lime juice • 2 tablespoons packed brown sugar •
1 tablespoon minced fresh mint • 1 tablespoon Asian sesame oil •
1½ teaspoons Chinese five-spice powder • One 3- to 4-pound chicken, cut into 8 pieces

Refreshing Cucumber Salad

SERVES SIX

This cool, cleanly flavored salad tempers the diverse and often powerful tastes of the other Asian dishes in this menu.

Halve the cucumbers lengthwise and scoop out the seeds. Cut crosswise into ¼-inch-thick slices. Place in a colander, sprinkle with 2 teaspoons of the salt, and toss to mix. Let drain for 15 minutes.

In a small saucepan, combine the sugar, the remaining 1 teaspoon salt, and the vinegar. Cook over medium heat, stirring occasionally, until the salt and sugar dissolve, about 2 minutes. Remove from the heat and let cool.

In a large bowl, combine the cucumbers, red onion, and cilantro. Pour the vinegar mixture over the cucumbers and toss well to coat. You can serve the salad immediately, but its flavor improves if you let it stand for 30 minutes to 1 hour before serving.

List *of* Ingredients

2½ pounds English (hothouse) cucumbers, peeled ·
3 teaspoons salt · 3 tablespoons sugar · ¾ cup rice vinegar · ½ red onion, thinly sliced ·
3 tablespoons fresh cilantro leaves

Coconut Rice

SERVES SIX AS A SIDE DISH

Coconut milk infuses the rice with a rich flavor that plays off the spicy-sweet characteristics of the other dishes in this menu.

In a medium saucepan, heat the oil over medium-high heat. Add the rice and cook, stirring, until the rice becomes translucent, about 2 minutes. Season with salt and pepper and stir in the coconut milk.

Bring to a boil, reduce the heat to low, cover, and cook until the liquid is absorbed, about 20 minutes. Fluff the rice with a fork, stir in the green onions, and let stand, covered, for 5 minutes before serving.

List *of* Ingredients

2 tablespoons peanut oil · 2 cups long-grain white rice ·
Salt and freshly ground pepper to taste · 4 cups canned unsweetened coconut milk ·
½ cup chopped green onions, including green parts

Smoky Green Beans

SERVES SIX AS A SIDE DISH

Smoked Chinese sausage and long beans are traditionally
used in this dish. If you can find these ingredients, by all means use them.
If not, kielbasa and green beans are perfectly acceptable alternatives.

In a large saucepan of salted boiling water, cook the green beans until crisp-tender, about 5 minutes. Drain the beans and rinse well with cold water. Drain and pat dry with paper towels.

In a small bowl, combine the chicken broth, rice wine, soy sauce, sesame oil, cornstarch, sugar, salt, and cayenne. Stir well; set aside.

In a wok or a large sauté pan, heat the canola oil over high heat until it shimmers. Add the ginger and garlic and stir-fry until crisp and brown, about 1 minute. Using a slotted spoon, remove the ginger and garlic from the wok and discard. Add the sausage pieces to the pan and stir-fry until crisp, about 2 minutes. Using the slotted spoon, transfer the sausage to paper towels to drain.

Add the green beans to the wok and stir-fry until the beans are tender and start to blister, 2 to 3 minutes. Return the sausage pieces to the pan and stir in the reserved sauce. Continue to cook until the sauce thickens, 1 to 2 minutes. Serve immediately.

List *of* Ingredients

2 pounds Chinese long beans or green beans, trimmed • ⅓ cup chicken broth •
1½ tablespoons Chinese rice wine (Shaoxing wine) • 1 tablespoon soy sauce • 1½ teaspoons Asian sesame oil •
1½ teaspoons cornstarch • ¾ teaspoon sugar • ½ teaspoon salt • ⅛ teaspoon cayenne pepper •
2 tablespoons canola or peanut oil • 3 fresh ginger slices, smashed with a knife • 3 garlic cloves, smashed with a knife •
6 ounces Chinese smoked sausage or kielbasa, cut into ¼-inch dice

Tropical Fruits Foster

SERVES SIX AS A DESSERT

Rum and butter highlight the sumptuous flavors of mango and pineapple
in this twist on the classic dessert traditionally made with bananas. The recipe serves
6 generously, because I know you'll swoon over this dessert as I do.

In a large, heavy skillet, melt the butter with the water over low heat. Add the pineapple wedges and cook, turning occasionally, until they begin to soften, about 5 minutes. Stir in the brown sugar and nutmeg and cook until the sugar dissolves. Add ⅓ cup of the rum, along with the mango and bananas, and cook for about 3 minutes, shaking the pan occasionally, until the fruit begins to brown and soften. Add the remaining ⅓ cup rum and cook for about 1 minute more. Using a long match, ignite the rum. Shake the pan until the flames subside, then remove the pan from the heat. Serve at once over vanilla ice cream.

List *of* Ingredients

½ cup (1 stick) unsalted butter • 2 tablespoons water •
Three ¾-inch-thick slices fresh pineapple, peeled, cored, and cut into 1-inch-thick wedges •
2 cups firmly packed brown sugar • ¼ teaspoon ground nutmeg • ⅔ cup dark rum • 1 mango, peeled, pitted,
and cut into 1-inch-thick wedges • 2 firm bananas, peeled and cut into ¾-inch-thick rounds •
6 scoops vanilla ice cream for serving

summer sensations

SHUCK corn, PICK tomatoes, SQUEEZE lemons,
CRACK lobster tails, MAKE a daisy chain, BREATHE IN the briny scent of the sea,
DANCE in a sun shower, SCATTER rose petals on your dinner table,
SIT on the porch, WAVE sparklers, PLANT honeysuckle, SIP champagne under
the stars, LICK an ice cream cone, HEAR the ocean in a shell,

have a summer fling with your senses every sultry day.

SUMMER CELEBRATIONS

In a rush of color, fragrance, and light, summer cascades in
through our windows and beckons us to live outdoors. This season of cookouts
and sand between the toes compels us to linger longer, whether we're pebble-skipping
on a pond or sharing secrets with a friend in the shade of a leafy tree.

Nature seems to hold its breath during these balmy months. After a spring season busy with growing, nature now simply *is*. We see purple delphiniums and bright hydrangeas. We hear waves at the shore or a katydid in the trees. We smell hot tar as we stroll to the farm stand or the ice cream shop—and we feel it, too, if we're lucky enough to be barefoot. We taste nature at its ripest, from sweet corn and heirloom tomatoes to Sugar May peaches and Queen Rosa plums, vegetables and fruits whose names are as sumptuous as their flavors.

Revel in this summer's beautiful bounty with style ideas including a flower-filled fireplace, a beach-pebble soap drainer, and lavender wands for scenting linen closets and clothing cupboards. Celebrate the season with an all-American Red, White, and Blueberry Breakfast (page 65) and an oh-so-continental Paella Party (page 77), showcasing summer's prize ingredients.

What will you linger over this summer? Why not wave a flag? Summer presents many opportunities for patriotic displays, from Flag Day on June 14 right through to Labor Day at the end of the season. In addition to hanging your flag with pride, there are lots of ways to bring the patriotic palette to your table. Use flag-motif ribbon for napkin ties. Make a flag cake: Bake a sheet cake, frost it with whipped cream, and place blueberries in the upper left for the stars and use strawberries for the red stripes. Make red, white, and blue sundaes with vanilla ice cream and blueberry sauce, topped with whipped cream and raspberries. Fashion a patriotic centerpiece from a bouquet of parade flags inserted in a blue spatterware pitcher.

Patriotic endeavors conjure up highfalutin notions such as victory, though in this case I speak of victory as in victory garden. When I was a kid, there was a show on our local public television station called *Victory Garden*. I thought the title derived from the gardening success you would enjoy if you were a loyal viewer of this program. Not so. In the 1940s, President

Franklin D. Roosevelt implored Americans to plant a victory garden and eat what they grew for reasons of thrift during the war. To my mind, this idea still has legs, not so much for thrift but for the fresh, succulent vegetables that will come forth. Radishes are the perfect candidates for a victory garden. They're easy to grow (involve your kids!), and they can be cultivated in the ground or in a container. Why not grow a bunch or two from seed? When they're ready for plucking, eat them as the French do, with sweet butter and salt. But before you do, admire their ruby hue and their peppery aroma. You'll enjoy them all the more.

Individual gestures punctuate the season, but group gatherings are as popular in summer as blueberries. Why not host a Red, White, and Blueberry Breakfast? Composed of favorite breakfast foods such as pancakes and sausage, but with a decided blueberry twist, it is a menu that does not tax the cook and allows for lingering around the table with the sports pages, tide tables, or the latest issue of *People* magazine. And since breakfast is not a seasonal activity, this menu is appropriate for any time of the year—simply substitute frozen blueberries when fresh aren't available.

The Spaniards have made lingering at the table an art. I speak from experience. When I lived in Spain, I spent many Sunday afternoons with my elbows on a table, laughing, conversing, and solving the world's problems over glasses of icy sangria, while children and dogs cavorted underfoot. What is it about close friends, unfettered laughter, and good food that makes everything seem easy? Try my Paella Party and let me know if you figure it out.

Robert Frost celebrated blueberries in his poem "Blueberries," admiring the wonder of these magnificent orbs of blue. You can do the same, every time you sip a refreshing glass of Blueberry Limeade (page 62).

Project *No.* One

SEASHELL ARRANGEMENT

Even if you don't live near the sea, you can still enjoy the timeless beauty of seashells. Look for them in craft shops as well as online. One of my favorite decorative accessories, seashells are especially sweet as containers for tiny flower arrangements. They'll brighten a summer table or powder room, or greet the "good morning" from a bedside nightstand: Fill the shell with well-soaked floral foam. Insert small blooms such as pansies, sweet peas, or jasmine.

Project *No.* Two

MIDSUMMER'S EVE SYLLABUB

Midsummer's Eve has been called "the high tide of the year" by the poet James Russell Lowell. Most Europeans mark this mid-point in the calendar, the summer solstice, on June 21, while the English celebrate it on June 24. Some people believe magic happens on this night. Why not celebrate by making a syllabub, a spirited dessert of fluffy whipped cream, sweet berries, and other delightful ingredients? The next day, wake up and dab your face with the morning dew. It's believed that doing so will make you more beautiful with each passing year (not that you need it).

serves six as a dessert the night before midsummer's day

³/₄ cup sweet Marsala wine · ²/₃ cup sugar · Grated zest and juice of 1 lemon · Grated zest and juice of 1 lime · 1 tablespoon vanilla extract · 1¹/₂ cups heavy cream, chilled · 1¹/₂ cups fresh berries such as raspberries and sliced strawberries · Edible flowers for garnish

In a medium bowl, combine all ingredients except the cream, berries, and flowers. Refrigerate for at least 1 hour or up to 4 hours.

Using an electric mixer, beat the mixture as you gradually add the heavy cream in a steady stream. When the mixture forms soft peaks, gently fold in the berries. Spoon into wineglasses or martini glasses. Refrigerate until ready to serve, up to 1 hour. Just before serving, decorate with edible flowers.

Project *No.* Three

HOSTESS WITH THE BLOOMING MOSTESS

Greet your guests this summer in high posy style. Using a craft glue, such as Sobo, glue silk flowers onto five-and-dime flip-flops. This is a fun project for kids and inexpensive enough to make for the entire family. Glue a few as party favors for your next gathering, too.

Project *No.* Four

FLOWER-FILLED FIREPLACE

Because it's usually the focal point of a room, you don't want your fireplace to be a black hole during the warm months when you aren't using it, do you? Put a wicker basket in it and fill the basket with a plant or flowers (in a waterproof container, of course). There are many interesting live grasses available that would be just right for such a display. You can also lay pretty white birch logs or place various-sized pillar candles on the log holder in the fireplace. At night, light the candles instead of a fire.

Project *No.* Five

CLIMBING VOTIVES

Outdoor lighting brings another dimension to outdoor entertaining. Turn empty baby food jars into hanging votives (if you don't have a little one, surely you know a new mom who would be happy to let you play recycler). Remove the labels with hot soapy water or Goo Gone, an adhesive remover. Wrap heavy florist wire around the neck of each jar, leaving enough at one end to make a hook for hanging. Insert a votive candle in each. Hang the votives along your porch or on trees. Or attach them to the rungs of a ladder for a climbing effect.

Project *No.* Six

LAVENDER WANDS

One of the first home air fresheners, lavender wands are an old English craft though nowadays they're found all over Provence. Summer is the time to make them. I like to put lavender wands in my linen closet as well as in my clothes closet and drawers, where their scent lasts for months, sometimes even years. Lavender is a known relaxant, so if you have trouble sleeping or are just plain stressed, put a lavender wand on your bedside table. They make wonderful gifts, too.

you will need:
20 freshly harvested lavender stems with buds · 1½ yards ¼-inch-wide satin ribbon

Remove all but 4 inches of buds from the stems. Gather the stems in your hand so the ends with the flower buds are even. Secure the stems by tying a piece of ribbon at the base of the buds, leaving 12 to 14 inches of ribbon on one end. Hold the bunch with the buds facing down and gently fold the stems down over the buds to encase them. Let the 12- to 14-inch ribbon tail fall into the lavender so the stems encase it, too. Beginning at the budded top of the wand, weave the remaining length of ribbon by going over 2 stems and then under 2 stems, alternating your way around the bunch. Weave tightly, as the wand will loosen as it dries. When all of the buds are woven with ribbon, wind the weaving ribbon around the bundle of stalks once or twice. Pick up the ribbon tail and use it with the weaving end to tie a tight knot. Wind both ends around the bundle to hide the knot and then tie them in a bow. Trim the stem ends.

Project *No.* Seven

ROSEWATER REFRESHER

On a hot or harried day, mist your face with rosewater. It refreshes your skin and revitalizes your spirits.

Gather 1 packed cup of unsprayed rose petals and put them in a heat-resistant bowl. Pour in 2 cups boiling water and cover. Let stand for 30 minutes. Strain the rosewater into a bottle or jug; discard the petals. Let the rosewater cool and then add 1 tablespoon of vodka. (The vodka acts as a preservative.) Cap the bottle or jar and store in the refrigerator, where it will keep for 4 to 6 weeks. Remember, this tonic is not meant to be ingested. Store it in a spray bottle so it's always ready for a spritz!

Project *No.* Nine

Project *No.* Eight

ROOT BEER FLOATS

A root beer float ranks right up there with other childhood summer pleasures such as campfire s'mores and long evenings spent playing capture the flag and kickball. Sip one and you'll see. Share a float with your kids. Maybe they'll sit still long enough to listen to your reminiscences.

Put a scoop of vanilla ice cream in a tall glass. Fill three-quarters full with root beer—the best you can find. Add another scoop of vanilla ice cream and top off with root beer. Heaven.

SIT AND SIP: BLUEBERRY LIMEADE

Balmy summer days call for a refreshing sip. This fragrant mix of zingy limes and mellow blueberries is just right for sharing with a friend. It makes wonderful popsicles, too. Plus, its color is beautiful to behold.

makes eight cups
1 cup sugar · 6 cups water · One 2-inch piece fresh ginger, peeled and sliced · 2 cups fresh or thawed frozen blueberries · 1 cup fresh lime juice (about 8 large limes) · Ice cubes for serving · Mint sprigs or lime twists for garnish

In a small saucepan, combine the sugar, water, and ginger. Cook over medium-high heat, stirring, until the sugar dissolves. Remove from the heat and let cool. Pour into a heatproof pitcher and refrigerate until cold, about 1 hour.

In a blender, combine the blueberries and the lime juice. Purée until smooth. Remove the ginger from the sugar syrup and discard. Pour the blueberry purée into the sugar syrup. Pour through a fine-mesh sieve to remove any blueberry skins. Serve over lots of ice garnished with mint or lime.

Project *No.* Ten

BEACH-PEBBLE DRAINER

Your children couldn't help themselves, so you've returned from your summer holiday with a veritable museum's worth of beach pebbles. Lucky you! They make perfect drainers for sponges and soaps. Put the pebbles into shallow bowls and station the drainers by your kitchen and bathroom sinks. Don't forget to pour out the excess water now and again.

RED, WHITE,
AND BLUEBERRY BREAKFAST

MENU

Nectarine-Ginger Pancakes *with* World's Easiest Blueberry Sauce

Blueberry Turkey Sausage Patties

Old-Fashioned Blueberry Muffins *with* Streusel Topping

Cherry-Blueberry Compote *with* Brown Sugar Mascarpone

More than any other berry, blueberries say "summer" to me.
When I was a child summering on Cape Cod, my sisters and I would join the line
of other blueberry enthusiasts at the kitchen door of Jonah's Inn waiting for
the first warm blueberry muffins to emerge from the oven.

A buxom, aproned woman with flour in her hair handed over the fruit-laden gems, which were bursting with berries and buttery flavor in equal measure. They were gone by the time we reached home, but the purple stains remained on our lips and fingertips well into the morning.

Sunday, with its relative tranquility, is the perfect day for a summer breakfast with blueberries as the highlight. The table is set outside on the porch with a vintage white tablecloth with lace trim and overlaid with a swath of homespun red ticking. Blue-edged enamelware plates and red-handled Bakelite flatware complete the breakfast-in-the-country motif. A big basket holds the day's newspapers for those who wish to indulge. Vintage milk bottles become containers for Blueberry Limeade (page 62), as well as vases for delphiniums and daisies from the garden.

Along with yummy blueberry muffins crowned with cinnamon streusel, the menu includes fluffy pancakes with blueberry sauce, blueberry turkey sausages, and a compote of berries with rich mascarpone. In a word, blueberrific!

Nectarine-Ginger Pancakes
with World's Easiest Blueberry Sauce

MAKES SIX TO EIGHT SERVINGS

The secrets to light and fluffy pancakes: Use buttermilk
and do not overmix. Lumps are a good thing. These pancakes are heady
with summer flavors, and they look pretty on the plate, too.

In a large bowl, whisk the flour, sugar, baking soda, and salt together. Make a well in the center of the mixture. Pour the eggs, buttermilk, ginger and juice, and the ¼ cup melted butter into the well. Whisking from the center and making your way outward, mix until the ingredients are combined but still a bit lumpy. Do not overmix.

Heat a griddle or large skillet over medium-high heat. Brush lightly with more melted butter. Ladle ¼ cupfuls of the pancake batter onto the griddle or skillet without letting them touch. Sprinkle the nectarine pieces on the tops of the pancakes, pressing them lightly into the batter.

After 2 to 4 minutes, when the pancakes begin to bubble in the center and the undersides are golden, flip them. Cook until the second side browns, about 1 minute. Transfer to a platter and keep warm in a 200°F oven. Add more butter to the pan and repeat to cook the remaining pancakes.

To make the sauce: In a small saucepan, combine all the ingredients. Bring to a simmer and cook until the berries are softened and some have burst, about 5 minutes.

List *of* Ingredients

3 cups all-purpose flour • ¼ cup sugar • 1 teaspoon baking soda • Pinch of salt •
2 eggs, lightly beaten • 2½ cups buttermilk • 2 teaspoons grated fresh
ginger with juice • 1¼ cup (½ stick) unsalted butter, melted, plus more for cooking pancakes •
2 ripe but firm nectarines, pitted and cut into ¼-inch dice

Blueberry Sauce: 2 cups best-quality maple syrup •
2 cups fresh or thawed frozen blueberries • 1 teaspoon ground cinnamon

Blueberry Turkey Sausage Patties

MAKES TWELVE PATTIES; SERVES SIX

Dried blueberries add a subtle tart note to these herby
sausage patties. If you can't find dried blueberries in your supermarket,
you can order them online from American Spoon Foods (www.spoon.com).
Alternatively, substitute dried cherries or cranberries
for the blueberries.

In a large bowl, combine all the ingredients except the oil. Stir well but do not overmix. Cover and refrigerate for at least 1 hour or as long as overnight.

Shape the turkey mixture into 12 patties, each about 2½ inches in diameter.

In a large skillet or on a griddle, heat the oil over medium heat. Arrange the patties in the skillet or on the griddle so they are not touching (you may have to cook them in 2 batches) and cook until browned, about 5 minutes on each side.

Serve immediately, or keep warm in a 200°F oven for up to 30 minutes.

List *of* Ingredients

1 pound ground white meat turkey · 8 ounces ground dark meat turkey ·
1 small onion, finely chopped · 1 cup dried blueberries · ¼ cup chopped fresh flat-leaf (Italian) parsley ·
1 egg, lightly beaten · 2 tablespoons dried bread crumbs · 2 tablespoons minced fresh sage ·
1 teaspoon grated lemon zest · 1 teaspoon salt · ½ teaspoon ground allspice ·
½ teaspoon ground pepper · 2 tablespoons olive oil

Old-Fashioned Blueberry Muffins *with* Streusel Topping

MAKES TWELVE MUFFINS

The crisp, crumbly, buttery streusel topping is the crowning glory
of these yummy, summery treats. A note of caution: If you use frozen blueberries,
do not thaw them first or they'll turn the batter blue.

Preheat the oven to 400°F. Grease a 12-cup standard muffin pan.

To make the streusel topping: In a food processor, combine the butter, sugar, and flour. Pulse until the mixture is the consistency of oatmeal. Transfer to a bowl and work the mixture with your hands until it will stick together when squeezed between your palms. The streusel should be lumpy so you'll have nice, big streusel crumbs on your muffins. Cover and refrigerate while you make the muffin batter.

To make the muffins: In a small bowl, whisk together the flour, baking powder, cinnamon, lemon zest, and salt. In another small bowl, combine the milk, heavy cream, and vanilla.

In a medium bowl, using an electric mixer set on medium speed, cream the butter and the sugar together until light and fluffy. Add the eggs one at a time, beating well after each addition and scraping down the sides of the

recipe continues on next page »

Old-Fashioned Blueberry
Muffins *with* Streusel Topping

continued

bowl, if necessary. With the mixer on the lowest speed, add the dry ingredients to the butter mixture in 2 additions, alternating with the milk mixture. Mix until just moistened. The batter will be lumpy. Gently fold in the blueberries, taking care not to break the fruit or to overmix.

Spoon the batter into each muffin cup, filling it level with the rim. Sprinkle each muffin with some of the streusel topping, dividing it evenly among the muffins.

Bake until golden and springy to the touch, or until a toothpick inserted into the center comes out clean, 20 to 25 minutes. Transfer the pan to a wire rack and let the muffins cool for 5 minutes before unmolding.

List *of* Ingredients

Streusel Topping: ½ cup (1 stick) cold unsalted butter,
cut into 8 pieces • ¼ cup packed light brown sugar • ¾ cup plus 2 tablespoons
all-purpose flour

Muffins: 2¼ cups all-purpose flour • 4 teaspoons baking powder •
1 teaspoon ground cinnamon • ½ teaspoon grated lemon zest • Pinch of salt • ½ cup
whole milk • ½ cup heavy cream • 2 teaspoons vanilla extract • ½ cup (1 stick) unsalted butter
at room temperature • ½ cup packed dark brown sugar • 2 eggs •
1½ cups fresh or frozen blueberries

Cherry-Blueberry Compote
with Brown Sugar Mascarpone

SERVES SIX

Though by no means essential, Italian maraschino
liqueur imparts a lovely sweetness to this compote. You can also
drizzle the liqueur over strawberries, add it to white wine for a cherry kir,
or sip it after dinner. A dollop of sweeetened mascarpone cheese
is a wonderfully rich finishing touch.

In a large serving bowl, combine the cherries and blueberries. Add the
lemon juice and toss gently. Add the granulated sugar and the liqueur (if
desired) and toss gently but thoroughly. Cover and refrigerate for at least
1 hour or up to 4 hours.

Stir the mascarpone and brown sugar together. Transfer to a small
serving bowl and serve alongside the fruit compote. Toss the fruit again
before serving.

List *of* Ingredients

4 cups fresh cherries, stemmed, halved, and pitted •
2 cups fresh blueberries • 2 tablespoons fresh lemon juice • $1/3$ cup granulated sugar •
¼ cup maraschino or other cherry liqueur (optional) • 2 cups mascarpone cheese
at room temperature • ¼ cup packed light brown sugar

PAELLA PARTY

MENU

Spanish Olives, Spanish-Style Marcona Almonds

Summer Salad *with* Sherry Vinaigrette

Tortilla *a la* Española

Basque Bell Pepper *and* Tomato Salad

Paella *a la* Valenciana

Spanish Sugar Cookies

Lemon *and* Orange Sorbets *in* Citrus Cups

Blushing Sangria

When I lived in Spain, I spent Sunday afternoons as the "ninth child"
of my friend Clara Maria Amezua de Llamas, at her spacious villa north of Madrid.
Like Clara Maria, paella is appealing, accessible, and authentically Spanish.
It's the perfect centerpiece for a celebration with family and friends.

Living in Spain reaffirmed for me what I had always known: Though we rush through the week, balancing personal and professional lives, Sundays really are meant for relaxation and rejuvenation. Reconnecting with family and friends nourishes our spirits, and a hearty, please-everybody dish such as paella satisfies our palates.

The menu for this get-together is all about ease. Olives and almonds can be purchased beforehand. The paella can be assembled almost entirely in the morning, except for the rice. Round out the paella with tapas—little dishes served with *aperitivos* in Spain—and salads. The traditional Tortilla a la Española, an egg and potato omelet, is substantial enough to be cut into wedges and is best served at room temperature. Basque Bell Pepper and Tomato Salad and a straight-forward green Summer Salad with Sherry Vinaigrette complement the paella. For dessert, serve lemon and orange sorbets. You can make them or purchase them; it's up to you. Scoop the sorbets into citrus shells for an authentically Spanish presentation. Pass *polvorones*, Spanish sugar cookies that melt in your mouth, at the table with the sorbets.

Serve this menu as a buffet, or family style at the table. Taking a cue from Spanish décor, I opted here for vivid colors and textural contrasts. Using the natural wood of my dining table as the "canvas," I set it with my collection of vibrant Mediterranean ceramics, including plates and tiles that act as coasters. Sunflower votives are made from fresh sunflowers (a variation of the project shown on page 20). Interspersed with the candles are cast-iron lanterns, evocative of those in the southern Mediterranean, filled with geraniums, the flower of Córdoba.

Greet your guests with a refreshing glass of sangria. Fiesta!

Summer Salad
with Sherry Vinaigrette

SERVES EIGHT AS A FIRST COURSE

Made in the warm, sunny south of Spain, sherry vinegar contributes
a sweet-tart note to this refreshing salad. The uncomplicated salad harmonizes
with the paella, which includes diverse ingredients and flavors. Feel free
to add other vegetables, including tomatoes, cucumbers, and bell peppers.

In a large salad bowl, whisk the olive oil, sherry vinegar, parsley, and garlic
together. Season with salt and pepper.

Just before serving, add the salad greens, oranges, mushrooms, and
red onion to the bowl and toss to coat with the vinaigrette.

List *of* Ingredients

Vinaigrette: ½ cup plus 2 tablespoons extra-virgin olive oil • 3 tablespoons
sherry vinegar • ¼ cup minced fresh flat-leaf (Italian) parsley • 2 large garlic cloves, minced •
Salt and freshly ground pepper to taste

Salad: About 12 cups salad greens • 2 small oranges,
peeled, halved, and thinly sliced • 6 ounces small white mushrooms,
cut into thin slices • ½ small red onion, thinly sliced

Tortilla *a la* Española

SERVES EIGHT AS A FIRST COURSE

This is the quintessential Spanish tapa, served in virtually
every bar in Spain. Really nothing more than a sturdy omelet, its basic
ingredients prove that simple things are often best.

In an 8- or 9-inch skillet, heat the oil over medium heat. Add the potato
slices to cover the bottom of the skillet. Do not overlap. Salt the potatoes,
then add a layer of onion slices and salt again. Repeat this process until you
have used up all the potatoes and onion. Cook slowly, gently turning the
potatoes, until they are tender but not brown. The potatoes should not
form a cake; they should remain separated. Drain the potatoes, reserving
2 tablespoons of the oil, and pat dry. Let cool.

Wipe out the skillet. Set the pan aside.

In a large bowl, beat the eggs until they are just foamy. Add a generous
pinch of salt. Add the potatoes to the beaten eggs, immersing them completely. Let the mixture stand at room temperature for 15 minutes.

Heat 1½ tablespoons of the reserved oil over medium-high heat until
it begins to smoke. Add the potato and egg mixture, spreading it out
quickly. Cook, shaking the pan constantly, until golden brown on the bottom, 2 to 3 minutes. Invert a plate over the skillet, turn the pan over, and
flip the tortilla out onto the plate. Add the remaining ½ tablespoon oil to
the skillet, then slide the tortilla into the skillet to brown on the other side,
2 minutes more.

Invert the plate over the skillet again and flip the tortilla onto the plate.
Let cool to room temperature.

To serve, cut into wedges or 1½-inch squares. Serve with crusty bread.

List *of* Ingredients

1 cup olive oil • 4 large baking potatoes, peeled and cut into ⅛-inch-thick slices •
Salt to taste • 1 large yellow onion, thinly sliced • 5 large eggs

Basque Bell Pepper *and* Tomato Salad

SERVES EIGHT AS A FIRST COURSE

The vibrant hues of the bell peppers, mingling with
the deep red of the tomatoes and a flash of lemon yellow, make this
refreshing salad from Spain's Basque region a wonderful addition
to a summer menu and a great complement to paella.

Cut the peppers into ½-inch-wide strips and arrange on a platter.
Sprinkle with salt. Arrange the tomatoes on top and sprinkle on the
chopped red onion. Add a bit more salt.

Before serving, drizzle with the olive oil and the red wine vinegar and
garnish with the lemon zest.

*Note on Roasting and Peeling Peppers: Preheat the oven to 450°F. Put the peppers in a
roasting pan and roast for 18 minutes on each side. Transfer to a paper bag and let cool
for 5 minutes. Peel, core, and seed them.*

List *of* Ingredients

6 bell peppers, in an assortment of colors, roasted and peeled (see note) •
Salt to taste • 4 tomatoes, diced • 1 small red onion, finely chopped • ¼ cup extra-virgin olive oil •
2 tablespoons red wine vinegar • Grated zest of 1 lemon

Paella *a la* Valenciana

SERVES EIGHT AS A MAIN COURSE

Paella takes its name from the two-handled shallow pan,
called a *paellera,* in which it is usually cooked. If you do not have such a pan, not to worry!
Use the biggest skillet you have on hand, or divide the mixture between
two skillets. This dish originated in Valencia, Spain (hence the name). It is festive,
impressive, sumptuous, easy to make, and perfect for a crowd!

In a paella pan or large ovenproof skillet, heat the olive oil over medium-high heat. Season the chicken with salt and pepper and cook until well browned and crisp, about 5 minutes per side. Using tongs, transfer the chicken to a plate. Add the sausages to the pan and cook until browned well on all sides, about 10 minutes. Transfer the sausages to the plate. Add the shrimp and cook for about 1½ minutes on each side, or until pink. Transfer the shrimp to the plate.

Add the onion, garlic, saffron, and tomatoes to the pan and cook, stirring occasionally, until the vegetables have softened, 5 to 7 minutes. Add the rice to the pan and stir to coat it well with the oil. Stir in 6 tablespoons of the parsley and the bay leaves. (The paella can be made in advance up to this point.)

recipe continues on page 86 »

Paella *a la* Valenciana

continued

Preheat the oven to 325°F. Stir the hot chicken broth, white beans, and green beans into the rice. Bring to a boil over medium-high heat. Cook, uncovered, stirring occasionally, for about 10 minutes. Return the chicken, sausage, and shrimp to the pan, burying them in the rice. Add the clams, pushing them into the rice, hinge side down. Decorate the paella with the roasted red pepper strips and peas. Put in the oven and bake, uncovered, for 20 minutes.

Remove from the oven and cover loosely with aluminum foil. Let stand for about 10 minutes. Remove any clams that do not open completely. While the paella rests, cook the squid tentacles in a large pot of boiling salted water for 1 minute or until opaque. Drain. Decorate the paella with the squid and lemon wedges and sprinkle with the remaining 2 tablespoons parsley. Serve immediately.

List *of* Ingredients

½ cup olive oil • 1 chicken, about 3 pounds, cut into 8 pieces • Salt and freshly ground pepper to taste • 3 chorizo or spicy Italian sausages, cut into ¾-inch pieces • 1½ pounds medium shrimp, shelled and deveined • 1 large yellow onion, chopped • 2 garlic cloves, minced • 1½ teaspoons saffron threads, crushed • One 28-ounce can peeled whole tomatoes, drained and chopped • 2½ cups short-grain white rice • 8 tablespoons chopped fresh flat-leaf (Italian) parsley • 2 bay leaves, crumbled • 4 cups chicken broth, heated • 2 cups cooked white beans such as cannellini • 8 ounces green beans, trimmed and cooked until crisp-tender • 24 clams (such as littlenecks), rinsed • 1 cup roasted red pepper strips (such as pimientos de piquillo), for garnish • 1 cup thawed frozen peas • ¼ pound squid tentacles, rinsed (optional) • 2 lemons, each cut into 4 wedges, for garnish

Spanish Sugar Cookies

MAKES ABOUT TWENTY-FOUR COOKIES

Spanish sugar cookies, or *polvorones*, are traditionally made with
confectioners', or powdered, sugar; *polvo* means "powder." While not cloyingly sweet,
the flavor and texture of these confections are phenomenal. You'll have a
difficult time limiting yourself to one. Since these cookies are very sugary (delightfully so),
you may wish to serve them in miniature paper cups, such as
those used for chocolates.

Preheat the oven to 325°F. In a small cup, stir the egg yolk and the 2 tablespoons sugar together. Stir in the brandy and set aside.

In a large bowl, using an electric mixer, beat the butter until light and fluffy. Beat in the egg yolk mixture until well combined.

With the mixer on its lowest setting, gradually add the flour to the butter mixture. The dough will be slightly sticky.

With floured hands, form balls of dough about 1 inch in diameter (about 1 tablespoon dough). Place on an ungreased baking sheet about 1 inch apart. Bake until firm but not browned, about 25 minutes. Transfer the cookies to wire racks and let cool for 2 to 3 minutes.

Place the 1½ cups confectioners' sugar on a sheet of parchment paper or waxed paper. Roll the warm cookies in the sugar, coating them on all sides. Return to the racks and let cool completely. Dust with some of the remaining confectioners' sugar.

List *of* Ingredients

1 egg yolk • 2 tablespoons confectioners' sugar, plus 1½ cups • 1 tablespoon brandy • 1 cup (2 sticks)
unsalted butter at room temperature • 2 cups all-purpose flour

Lemon *and* Orange Sorbets *in* Citrus Cups

SERVES EIGHT AS A DESSERT

At once refreshing and pretty, these sorbets in citrus cups are served
in both Spain and Italy. They are the perfect ending for a summer meal. A serrated-edge
grapefruit spoon makes quick work of scooping out the citrus cups.

To make the lemon sorbet: In a small, heavy saucepan, combine the water
and sugar. Bring to a boil over medium-high heat and cook, stirring occasionally, until the sugar dissolves and the mixture is clear, 1 to 2 minutes.

Remove the syrup from the heat, add the lemon zest, and let stand for
20 minutes. Pour the lemon juice and Limoncello (if using) into the syrup.
Cover and refrigerate until chilled, about 2 hours.

Pour the mixture into an ice-cream maker and process according to the
manufacturer's instructions. Transfer to a freezer-safe container. Cover
and freeze until firm, at least 3 hours.

To make the orange sorbet: Follow the directions for the lemon sorbet.

Cut a very small piece (about ⅛ inch thick) from the bottom of each fruit so
it will stand upright. Do not pierce the flesh. Cut off the tops of the fruits and
set aside. (These will be the "lids.") Using a teaspoon or a grapefruit spoon,
scoop out the flesh from the fruits so only the rind remains; reserve the flesh
for another use. Freeze the citrus tops and cups until firm, about 1 hour.

Scoop the sorbets into the citrus cups and freeze until ready to serve.
To serve, cover each of the citrus cups with its top.

List *of* Ingredients

Lemon Sorbet: 1½ cups water • 1¼ cups sugar • 1 heaping tablespoon grated
lemon zest • 1½ cups lemon juice (from about 6 large lemons) • 2 tablespoons Limoncello (page 22; optional)

Orange Sorbet: 1½ cups water • 1 cup sugar • 1 heaping tablespoon grated
orange zest • 1½ cups orange juice (from about 5 large oranges) • 2 tablespoons orange liqueur (optional)

4 large lemons • 4 oranges

Blushing Sangria

MAKES ABOUT EIGHT CUPS

This Spanish mixture of iced wine and fruit makes a refreshing summer beverage. I substituted rosé wine for the red wine that is traditionally used to make sangria because I like its lighter flavor. You can also use white wine. And by all means, vary the fruit according to what's on hand and what suits your whim.

In a pitcher, combine the orange and lemon slices, plum and peach wedges, strawberries, grapes, and lemon juice. Sprinkle with the sugar and toss to combine. Add the orange liqueur and let stand at least 1 hour. Stir in the 1 cup orange juice and the wine. Add more orange juice to taste, if you like. Refrigerate for 1 to 2 hours, or until chilled.

List *of* Ingredients

1 orange, sliced and seeded · 1 lemon, sliced and seeded ·
2 plums, pitted and cut into ½-inch wedges · 1 peach, pitted and cut into ½-inch wedges ·
6 strawberries, halved · 6 seedless grapes, halved · 2 tablespoons fresh lemon juice · 2 tablespoons
granulated sugar · ¼ cup orange liqueur such as Grand Marnier · 1 cup fresh orange juice,
plus more as needed · One 750-ml bottle chilled rosé wine

autumn sensations

PICK apples, GATHER colorful leaves, CARVE a jack-o'-lantern,

MEANDER down a country lane, MAKE cinnamon toast, STACK firewood,

CRACK walnuts, PEEL a tangerine, LISTEN to the wind,

SIP mulled cider, ROOT for your favorite football team, INHALE the

aroma of apple crisp, GIVE thanks,

indulge in an idyll with your senses each brisk autumn day.

AUTUMN CELEBRATIONS

From crimson in the trees to crispness in the wind, autumn ignites
the natural world. This season of tailgate picnics and
leaves crackling underfoot urges us to recognize time's ephemeral
quality and to treasure each moment.

Just as a rose smells sweetest right before its demise, autumn flaunts its fleeting nature. We see sunshine dappling on golden grasses. We hear the wind rustling through the trees, their branches becoming barer with each passing day. We feel the pleasant softness of well-worn flannel shirts. We taste the tartness of just-picked pippin apples and the cinnamon laced into the crumble we make with them.

Celebrate autumn's riotous colors and rich textures in your home with walnut salt and pepper cellars (perfect for your Thanksgiving table), copper oak leaves that will last all year long, and a centerpiece made quick-as-a-wink with persimmons and quince. And celebrate the season at your table with a sampler of warming, nourishing soups just right for a Sunday supper with the family or a Saturday dinner with friends. Commemorate special occasions of autumn, such as birthdays, with a yellow butter cake covered with luxurious buttercream frosting.

How will you spend your time this autumn? Perhaps you'll conjure up ideas for displaying those charming purchases you made at summer flea markets and antique shows. Don't relegate them to a cupboard. Give them an honored place in a much-used room, like the kitchen, so you can enjoy them every day. Pitchers make wonderful utensil holders. Roll napkins or dish towels and arrange them in baskets. Group candlesticks in a corner of the kitchen (light the candles every night!). Transform flower frogs into pencil or candle holders. Sip from the teacups you've been collecting for years.

As you're ruminating over the possibilities, wrap yourself in a cozy quilt or blanket. Aside from their inherent abilities to bring warmth and comfort, blankets have become fashionable of late, especially those with pedigree. Quintessential American blankets include striped Beacon and plaid Pendleton, and Swans Island blankets with gorgeous colors and patterns made by the Atlantic Blanket Company. Keep your eyes open for them when you visit Aunt Millicent's lake cabin this summer or Grandma Kitty's house this Thanksgiving. If you hone in on one, pat it gently, smile sweetly and say, "You know, I've always admired . . ." Bingo!

Autumn colors extend to the season's vegetables, too. Use them to make soups for a supper gathering that includes an autumn minestrone with tiny meatballs. It's a crowd—as in adults *and* kids—pleaser. Purchase extra vegetables and fruits at the farmers' market so you can decorate the table with them, too. They're simple yet stunning in their presentation.

Autumn's chilly weather prompts warm, intimate indoor gatherings. It's always good to spend time with those we love. If there is a reason to gather for a cozy meal, all the better. This is why I created the Autumn Birthday Celebration (page 123). It's an unpretentious event, buoyed by food everybody loves, such as chicken potpie. Of course, this menu can be served for any special occasion: Your child scored a goal in her soccer game. Your friend finally got up the nerve to ask out someone at work. Autumn is here!

This section will inspire you to spend time in sensory endeavors that celebrate the season. Whether you decorate or admire, cook or consume, fall into it with abandon!

Project *No.* One

SIT AND SIP: CARDAMOM COFFEE

I learned this from a Scandanavian friend: Before brewing coffee in a drip coffeemaker, insert a cardamom pod in the filter bag with the coffee. The cardamom will imbue the coffee with its exotic perfume. This coffee is delish.

Project *No.* Two

PUMPKIN PAGEANT

Jack-o'-lanterns rule the porch rail on Halloween, their menacing visages winking and blinking at trick-or-treaters. Decorated pumpkins deserve a place, too. Embark on an autumn ramble through woods and fields and collect seed pods, leaves, small pinecones, and other natural treasures. Add seashells, beads, twine, and other around-the-house finds to your supply arsenal. Now, grab a glue gun and create pumpkin personalities from your collection of decorations. These pumpkin "people," while not glimmering at night, will contribute glamour to the daytime porch or dining table. And decorating pumpkins is safer for kids than carving.

Project *No.* Three

GOURD DOORSTOP

It may still be warm outside, but autumn's brisk breezes can slam a door faster than you can say "Peter, Peter, Pumpkin Eater." So, press a pumpkin or gourd into doorstop service. Either will be heavy enough to hold the door and pretty enough to please your eye.

Project *No.* Four

COPPER FOIL OAK LEAVES

These autumn leaves will last through the season and beyond. Gather oak (or another variety) leaves. Place a sheet of 1.5-millimeter-thick copper foil on the top of a leaf. Gently rub the copper foil with a Foilmate (foiling tool) or rubber burnisher to bring out the leaf shape, along with its veins and overall texture. Cut the leaf shape from the foil. Copper oak leaves can be affixed to wreaths, used as napkin adornments or place cards, or displayed on a bookshelf or mantel.

Project *No.* Five

MOSS CANDLESCAPE

To illuminate autumn's rustic character, fill a wooden bowl or bucket with soil, top with damp moss, and nestle candles within. Votive candles in glass holders are especially nice. If you wish, accent the presentation with small branches, rocks, and other natural elements.

Project *No.* Six

PUTTING UP

"Putting up" is an old-fashioned way to say "preserving." In the olden days, one of the homemaker's main tasks was to put up, or preserve, fruits and vegetables every summer and autumn so that they would be available during the winter months. There is something inherently satisfying about preserving. Rows of jars filled with applesauce or tomato sauce lined up on my kitchen counter make me smile. And when I give a jar to friends, it makes them smile, too. Why not spend an autumn afternoon putting up cinnamon applesauce? And since it's made with unpeeled red-skinned apples, it's pink! Give jars to your Thanksgiving guests or to your children's teachers as holiday gifts, but don't forget to keep some for yourself.

Project *No.* Seven

CINNAMON APPLESAUCE

makes about eight half-pints
16 unpeeled red-skinned apples such as MacIntosh or Rome Beauty,
cored and quartered · 1¼ cups fresh lemon juice (about 8 lemons) · ½ cup sugar ·
Two 4-inch cinnamon sticks, broken in half · 2 cups water

Put the apples in a large, heavy saucepan. Sprinkle them with the lemon juice and toss thoroughly to coat. Add the sugar, cinnamon sticks, and water. Bring to a boil, then immediately reduce the heat to medium-low. Cover the pot and let simmer until the apples break down to applesauce, 30 to 40 minutes. Remove from the heat, uncover, and let the apples cool slightly in the pot. Discard the cinnamon sticks. Using a rubber scraper, gently push the apples through a coarse-mesh sieve or food mill. Discard the peels.

Return the applesauce to the pot and heat until it begins to bubble. Transfer to hot, sterilized jars. Seal and store in the refrigerator for up to 2 weeks.

Project *No.* Eight

PERSIMMONS AND QUINCE

Gather the most beautiful orange persimmons and green-speckled quince from an orchard, roadside stand, or supermarket produce section, then arrange them in a garden trug, a green-glazed pottery bowl, or a porcelain compote. The vessel you select will determine the effect, from casual to oh, so elegant. Plus, the aroma of the quince will perfume an entire room.

Project *No.* Nine

BLANKET BLISS

A cozy quilt or blanket, in the colors of autumn, will brighten dark days and provide warmth on chilly nights. It's also a lovely way to bring the season into your home décor. When I am browsing tag sales and antique shops, I keep my eyes peeled for vintage blankets with interesting colors and patterns. When autumn comes, I take them out and place them throughout the house, over the arm of a chair by the fireplace, across the end of the guestroom bed, on the ottoman in the den, on the sofa in my office. They look pretty, and they're always at the ready to warm cold toes.

Project *No.* Ten

WALNUT SALT AND PEPPER CELLARS

When the grandparents descend upon your home for an extended autumn visit, corral them into making walnut salt and pepper cellars for the Thanksgiving table. Using a nutcracker, crack a walnut in half. With a nut pick or cocktail fork, hollow out the nut and any detritus that remains. Fill each half with salt and pepper. Allot one set per dinner guest. Everybody will be enchanted.

Project *No.* Eleven

DRIED APPLES AND PEARS

No one seems to tire of a visit to the fruit orchard on an autumn afternoon. Is it the beauty of the trees? The satisfaction of biting into a fresh-from-the-branch Rome Beauty apple or Bosc pear? The thrill of climbing a ladder to reach the highest fruit? When you return home, flushed from the chilly air and satisfied with your effort, why not preserve those memories and dry some of the fruit? Here's how: Cut the apples or pears lengthwise into fairly thick slices, about ¼ inch. Dip the slices into a solution of equal parts lemon juice and water. Place on baking sheets lined with parchment paper. Dry in a 150°F oven (200°F if your oven will go only that low) for 4 to 6 hours, leaving the door slightly ajar. Let cool completely. Pack in airtight tins or boxes, separating each layer with parchment paper, for up to 1 month.

Project *No.* Twelve

SPRING BULBS

Autumn is the time to plant spring-flowering bulbs. It's a fun activity to do with children. Choose your crocuses, daffodils, hyacinths, and tulips from a garden catalog or from your local nursery. To ensure a beautiful display, group the bulbs into irregular patterns of fifteen or more. This way, the flowers will come up in gorgeous drifts. Place the bulbs, pointy side up, at a depth equal to 3 times their diameter and fill the holes with soil. Now you can look forward to a spring morning when you'll see the first show of green peeping up through the soil (or snow).

SOUP FOR SUPPER

MENU

Cheese Sampler *with* Autumn Fruits *and* Nuts

Autumn Salad *with* Persimmons *and* Pecans

Wild Mushroom Topping *for* Crusty Bread

Autumn Minestrone *with* Tiny Turkey Meatballs

Cape Cod Clam Chowder

Chestnut Soup *with* Black Pepper Cream

Three-Apple Crisp

A good soup can transform a meal into a
nourishing and satisfying experience. I especially like to make soup in the autumn,
when root vegetables are available to lend their earthy flavor to the soup
pot and their rustic colors and shapes to the table.

This is an everyday celebration that can take place any day during the week, with your family or a larger group. If you're cooking for the former, you may want to choose just one soup. The Autumn Minestrone with Tiny Turkey Meatballs is a real kid-pleaser and tastes even better when made in advance.

If you're hosting others and preparing all three soups, you have a choice when it comes to serving them. Set up a buffet in the kitchen with an array of cheeses and seasonal fruits and nuts, and invite guests to help themselves, or go the seated-and-served route and offer a "flight of soups." Use small cups or bowls, and serve the clam chowder first, followed by the minestrone and, finally, the chestnut soup. Alternatively, you can set the three cups on chargers and serve them all at once. Put a bowl of Autumn Salad with Persimmons and Pecans at each end of the table, along with baskets of crusty, warm bread. At each setting, place a ramekin of Wild Mushroom Topping. I like to serve a variety of crackers, too, from oyster crackers and goldfish to RyKrisp and saltines. For dessert, serve a warm apple crisp with vanilla ice cream and caramel sauce.

Your table should reflect the season's vivid hues and natural bounty. I nestled autumn fruits and vegetables among leafy branches in the center of the table, with votive candles in jewel-toned holders. Natural linen napkins, along with gray-green drabware and amber wineglasses, complement the rustic elegance of the table decoration as well as the menu. As for those cups—enough for three soups!—don't despair. Employ coffee mugs, teacups, or tempered glass tumblers, or borrow from others. It's fun to mix up the presentation.

Autumn Salad *with* Persimmons *and* Pecans

SERVES EIGHT AS A FIRST COURSE

There are two varieties of persimmons; the larger, heart-shaped Hachiya,
which is ripe when very soft, and the short, squat Fuyu persimmon, whose crisp flesh
adds sweetness and color to this salad. If you've never tried a persimmon,
an often-overlooked fruit, now's the time.

In the bottom of a salad bowl, combine the vinegar and honey with a generous pinch of salt. Gradually whisk in the walnut oil. Season with the pepper and more salt, if desired.

Tear the lettuce leaves into bite-sized pieces and add them to the salad bowl along with the persimmons, pecans, and dried cherries. Toss well to coat. Serve immediately.

Note on Toasting Nuts: Preheat the oven to 325°F. Place the nuts on a baking sheet in a single layer. Toast until fragrant, 10 to 15 minutes, shaking the pan every few minutes to prevent scorching.

List *of* Ingredients

3 tablespoons Champagne vinegar or white wine vinegar • 2 teaspoons honey •
Salt to taste • ⅔ cup walnut oil • Freshly ground white pepper to taste • Leaves from 2 heads red oakleaf lettuce
or other leaf lettuce • 2 Fuyu persimmons, peeled and cut into thin wedges • 1 cup pecans,
toasted and coarsely chopped (see note) • ¾ cup dried sweet cherries

Wild Mushroom Topping *for* Crusty Bread

SERVES EIGHT AS AN APPETIZER OR SIDE DISH

Chewy, crusty artisanal bread is heaven on its own. Topped with this warm
wild mushroom spread, it is stellar. When you're not enjoying the
wild mushrooms on bread, you might try them on steak or polenta, or use them
to fill miniature tart shells for an extraordinary hors d'oeuvre. Yum.

Put the dried mushrooms in a small bowl and add hot water to cover. Let
stand for 30 minutes.

In a large sauté pan, heat the olive oil over medium-low heat. Add the
onion and garlic and cook, stirring, until softened. Drain the mushrooms,
reserving the liquid. Chop the mushrooms and add to the pan along with
the fresh mushrooms. Increase heat to high and cook, stirring, until the
fresh mushrooms soften. Add the wine and all but the last ¼ inch of
the reserved mushroom soaking liquid. Bring to a boil, reduce the heat to
low, and simmer for 20 minutes. Add the cream, lemon juice, and parsley and
season generously with salt and pepper. Serve warm or at room temperature.

List *of* Ingredients

2 ounces dried wild mushrooms such as porcini or chanterelles • 2 tablespoons extra-virgin olive oil •
1 large yellow onion, finely chopped • 4 garlic cloves, minced • 2 pounds assorted fresh mushrooms, such as oysters,
shiitakes, and white mushrooms, coarsely chopped (stem shiitakes) • ½ cup dry Marsala wine •
¼ cup heavy cream • Juice of 1 lemon (about 2 tablespoons) • ¼ cup chopped fresh flat-leaf (Italian) parsley •
Salt and freshly ground pepper to taste

Autumn Minestrone
with Tiny Turkey Meatballs

SERVES EIGHT AS A MAIN COURSE

The ingredients list may look daunting, but the preparation is a piece of cake
(or spoonful of soup, as it were). Parsnips, which are quintessential autumn vegetables,
lend sweetness and another flavor dimension. And kids love the tiny meatballs!
Make a few extra so you can spoon them out of the simmering soup and treat your
little ones to them as they run through the kitchen.

In a Dutch oven or soup pot, heat the olive oil over medium heat. Add the onion, carrots, celery, and parsnip and cook, uncovered, until softened, about 8 minutes. Stir in the garlic and cook just until fragrant, about 1 minute. Add the Swiss chard and cook until wilted, about 1 minute. Add the chicken broth, wine, tomato, and bay leaf and bring to a boil. Reduce the heat to low, cover, and simmer for 1 hour. During the last 10 minutes of cooking, add the chickpeas, basil, and parsley. Season with salt and pepper. Discard the bay leaf.

recipe continues on next page »

Autumn Minestrone *with* Tiny Turkey Meatballs

continued

While the soup simmers, make the meatballs: In a medium bowl, combine the turkey, cheese, bread crumbs, sage, parsley, salt, and pepper. Add the egg and mix until just incorporated. Cover and refrigerate until ready to cook.

After the soup has simmered for 1 hour, increase the heat to medium and bring to a gentle boil. Use a tablespoon to form the meatballs and, as you do so, drop them into the soup. Cover the soup and cook until the meatballs are cooked through, about 12 minutes.

Serve hot. Pass Parmesan cheese at the table.

List *of* Ingredients

2 tablespoons olive oil • 1 yellow onion, coarsely chopped •
2 carrots, peeled and sliced ½ inch thick • 2 celery stalks, sliced ½ inch thick • 1 parsnip, peeled and sliced
½ inch thick • 2 garlic cloves, minced • 3 cups chopped Swiss chard leaves • 4 cups chicken broth • 1 cup dry red wine •
1 large tomato, seeded and chopped into 1-inch pieces • 1 bay leaf • One 15-ounce can chickpeas, drained •
¼ cup chopped fresh basil • 2 tablespoons minced fresh flat-leaf (Italian) parsley •
Salt and freshly ground pepper to taste

Tiny Turkey Meatballs: 8 ounces ground white meat turkey • 8 ounces ground
dark meat turkey • ⅓ cup freshly grated Parmesan cheese • 3 tablespoons dried bread crumbs •
½ teaspoon chopped fresh sage • 2 tablespoons minced fresh flat-leaf
(Italian) parsley • ½ teaspoon salt • ½ teaspoon freshly ground pepper • 1 egg, beaten •
Freshly grated Parmesan cheese for serving

Cape Cod Clam Chowder

SERVES EIGHT

Fresh clams really do make a difference when it comes to making
clam chowder from scratch. Their briny sweetness rounds out the smoky bacon and
the flinty wine. The addition of corn adds color as well as a pleasant crunch.
I like to serve this when it's cold and rainy outside because it reminds me of warm
summer days at the shore.

Discard any cracked or open clams. In a large pot, melt 2 tablespoons of
the butter over low heat. Add the garlic and sauté until it begins to soften,
1 to 2 minutes. Add the bay leaf, water, and wine. Increase the heat and
bring to a boil. Reduce the heat to low, add the clams, cover, and steam just
until they open, 5 to 8 minutes, depending on their size.

Line a colander with cheesecloth and place over a large bowl. Drain the
clams, discarding any unopened ones. Reserve the strained liquid.

Rinse out the pot. Add the remaining 2 tablespoons butter and place
the pot over medium heat. Add the pancetta and cook just until it begins to
brown.

Add the leeks and sauté until they soften, about 3 minutes. Sprinkle the flour over the leeks and cook, stirring, for 1 minute.

Stirring constantly, pour in the reserved clam liquid and the half-and-half. When the liquid boils, reduce the heat to a simmer. Add the potatoes and thyme and cook until the potatoes are tender, about 15 minutes.

Remove the clams from the shells, reserving a few in their shells for garnish. When the potatoes are tender, add the shelled clams and the corn and simmer for 1 to 2 minutes more. Season with salt and pepper. Serve hot, garnished with the chopped chives and parsley and a whole clam or two.

List *of* Ingredients

48 clams in the shell, scrubbed · 4 tablespoons unsalted butter ·
2 garlic cloves, minced · 1 bay leaf · 3 cups water · 3 cups dry white wine · 8 ounces pancetta or lean bacon,
coarsely chopped · 2 leeks, including tender green portions, rinsed and thinly sliced ·
1 tablespoon all-purpose flour · 4 cups half-and-half · 4 unpeeled red potatoes, cut into ½-inch dice ·
1 teaspoon ground thyme · 2 cups fresh or thawed frozen corn kernels · Salt and freshly ground pepper to taste ·
2 tablespoons minced fresh chives or green onions (green part only) ·
2 tablespoons minced fresh flat-leaf (Italian) parsley

Chestnut Soup
with Black Pepper Cream

SERVES EIGHT AS A MAIN COURSE

Though they are the lowest in fat of all the nuts,
chestnuts contribute an earthy flavor and rich texture to any dish they grace.
This soup is worth making for its aroma alone (close your eyes and you're
in a chestnut grove in Italy), but you'll like the taste, too.

Heat oven to 450°F. Score chestnuts with an "X" on the flat sides of their shells, and arrange them "X" sides up on a baking sheet. Roast until shells begin to peel back from nuts, 4 to 5 minutes.

Remove chestnuts from oven, and let rest until cool enough to handle. Peel and discard shells.

Fill a medium saucepan with water and bring to a boil over medium-high heat. Working in batches, blanch chestnuts until their brown skins begin to loosen, 1 to 2 minutes. Remove chestnuts and drain on a paper towel–lined baking sheet. When cool enough to handle, peel off skins.

In a medium saucepan, heat the oil over medium heat. Add the onions, reduce the heat to low, and cook until onions are soft and just beginning to color, about 10 minutes. Add the potatoes, chestnuts, and the 6 cups chicken broth and cook until vegetables and nuts are soft, about 30 minutes.

recipe continues on next page »

Chestnut Soup *with* Black Pepper Cream

continued

In a blender or food processor, purée the soup in batches until it is smooth but with a bit of texture. Season with salt and pepper. If the soup is too thick for your liking, add more broth. Return to the saucepan and heat through.

To make the black pepper cream: In a small bowl, stir the crème fraîche and heavy cream together until smooth. Stir in the pepper.

Serve hot, garnished with a dollop of the black pepper cream topped with a thyme sprig.

List *of* Ingredients

1 pound chestnuts • 2 tablespoons olive oil • 3 large onions, coarsely chopped •
4 red potatoes, peeled and coarsely chopped • 6 cups chicken broth, plus more as needed •
Salt and freshly ground pepper to taste

Black Pepper Cream: ¼ cup crème fraîche or sour cream • ¼ cup heavy cream •
2 teaspoons freshly ground pepper • Fresh thyme sprigs for garnish

Three-Apple Crisp

SERVES EIGHT AS A DESSERT

This old-fashioned dessert is the perfect ending to a homey meal.
It's made with three varieties of apples, each of which adds its own taste and texture,
and molasses for depth of flavor. Vanilla ice cream and caramel sauce
complete the delicious picture. Accompany it with Cardamom Coffee (page 97).

Preheat the oven to 400°F. In a medium bowl, toss the apples with the molasses and lemon juice. In another bowl, combine the oats, brown sugar, flour, spices, and salt. Using a pastry blender or 2 dinner knives, cut in the butter until the mixture resembles coarse crumbs and the dough just barely holds together.

Spoon the apples into a 9-by-13-inch baking dish and spoon the dry mixture over it. Bake until the topping is brown and crisp, about 10 minutes. Reduce the heat to 350°F and bake until the fruit is bubbling, 30 to 35 minutes more. Serve with vanilla ice cream and caramel sauce.

List *of* Ingredients

6 apples, 2 each of 3 varieties, such as pippin, Rome Beauty, and Granny Smith,
peeled, cored, and cut into chunks • ¼ cup molasses • 2 tablespoons fresh lemon juice • ½ cup rolled oats •
¾ cup lightly packed dark brown sugar • ²/₃ cup all-purpose flour • 1 teaspoon ground cinnamon •
½ teaspoon ground allspice • ¼ teaspoon salt • 6 tablespoons unsalted butter •
Vanilla ice cream for serving • Caramel sauce for serving

AUTUMN BIRTHDAY
CELEBRATION

MENU

Roasted Beets *with* Blue Cheese *and* Walnuts

Spinach Salad *with* Shallot Vinaigrette

Chicken Potpie

Velvet Birthday Cake *with* Vanilla Buttercream Frosting

Chances are you know somebody who has an autumn birthday.
This seasonal celebration is for them, or anyone else celebrating a special event.

It's an unpretentious dinner for a quiet evening with family and close friends, featuring good food and relaxed conversation. This celebration is particularly nice for people, like my husband, who appreciate thought and creativity but loathe zealous displays of attention.

The dinner menu reflects the relaxed mood and easy camaraderie of this get-together. The food is simple but special, because it's homemade: chicken potpie crowned with a Cheddar cheese crust, roasted beets with blue cheese and walnuts, and a velvety yellow cake covered with drifts of rich buttercream frosting. You can make the potpie filling a day in advance. Bake the cake layers a few days before the party, wrap them well, and freeze. Bring the layers to room temperature before frosting the cake.

A birthday, like many commemorative occasions, involves numbers. My version of this dinner has a numerical theme. Each place setting is marked with enameled-metal house numbers, and the napkins are tied with lengths of cloth tape measure. Billiard balls, with their festive colors and graphic numbers, hold vibrant dahlias in a clear glass globe. Rosemary and other supple branches are wired into numerals depicting the birthday boy's age and suspended over the table.

In Spain, where I once lived, it's customary for the birthday celebrant to buy dinner for his friends. In the spirit of this generosity, I slip numeral-shaped cookies, cut from refrigerated sugar-cookie dough, into muslin bags stamped with the birthday honoree's name and age and bestow the bags as party favors. When it's time to make a wish, do as the Spanish do and ask everybody to slide their rings onto the birthday candles. When the guest of honor blows out the candles, everyone makes a wish on his or her ring.

Roasted Beets
with Blue Cheese *and* Walnuts

SERVES SIX AS A FIRST COURSE OR SIDE DISH

Sweet and tart, rich and refreshing, and definitely a colorful addition to the menu,
this is one of my favorite dishes. Sometimes I serve it as a first course, other times as a side dish.
And it works either way for this menu, too. Be sure to dress the beets with the
vinaigrette while they're still warm so they'll absorb the flavor.

Preheat the oven to 400°F. In a small bowl, combine the vinegars, salt, and pepper. Whisk until blended. Stir in the orange zest. Slowly whisk in the olive oil. Taste and adjust the seasoning. Set aside.

Wrap the beets individually in aluminum foil and place in a roasting pan. Bake until they are tender when pierced with a knife, about 1½ hours. Transfer to a wire rack and let cool to the touch. Remove the foil, slip off the skins, and cut the beets crosswise into ¼-inch-thick slices.

While the beets are still warm, toss them with ¾ cup of the vinaigrette. Using a slotted spoon, transfer to a serving bowl. Crumble the blue cheese over them. Drizzle with the remaining vinaigrette and sprinkle with the walnuts. Serve warm or at room temperature.

List *of* Ingredients

3 tablespoons balsamic vinegar · 1 tablespoon red wine vinegar ·
½ teaspoon salt · ¼ teaspoon freshly ground pepper · 2 tablespoons freshly grated
orange zest · 1 cup extra-virgin olive oil · 6 golden or red beets or a combination
(1½ to 2 pounds total), stems trimmed to 1 inch · 8 ounces semisoft blue cheese such as
Maytag or Danish blue · 1 cup coarsely chopped walnuts

Spinach Salad
with Shallot Vinaigrette

SERVES SIX AS A FIRST OR THIRD COURSE

This unadorned salad is the ideal foil to the multilayered
flavors of the chicken potpie. I like to serve it as a third course, after the potpie.
It refreshes the palate and readies it for the sweet dessert to come.

In a salad bowl, combine the vinegar, mustard, salt, and pepper. Whisking
constantly, add the olive oil in a slow, steady stream. Stir in the shallots.
Taste and adjust the seasoning. Just before serving, add the spinach leaves
and toss to coat.

List *of* Ingredients

2 tablespoons red wine vinegar · 2 tablespoons Dijon mustard ·
½ teaspoon salt · ¼ teaspoon freshly ground pepper · 6 tablespoons extra-virgin olive oil ·
¼ cup minced shallots · 10 cups baby spinach leaves

Chicken Potpie

SERVES SIX AS A MAIN COURSE

Savory chunks of chicken and vegetables in a creamy sauce,
topped by a crunchy Cheddar-laced biscuit crust, make this potpie a
gift in itself. Sure, it will take you a little time to prepare,
but the results are worth it. The guest of honor will remember
this meal. I guarantee it.

Preheat the oven to 400°F.

To make the crust: In a medium bowl, stir the flour, cheese, rosemary, and salt together. Using a pastry blender or 2 dinner knives, cut in the butter and shortening until the mixture resembles coarse meal. Gradually stir in the milk until the dough clumps together. Turn out onto a lightly floured work surface and press into a disk. Wrap the dough in plastic wrap and refrigerate for 30 minutes.

To make the filling: In a medium saucepan, melt the butter over medium-high heat. Add the carrots, potato, and leeks and cook, stirring, until the leeks are softened, about 5 minutes. Sprinkle in the flour and cook, stirring, for 1 minute. Stir in the broth, wine, and half-and-half and bring to a simmer. Cover, reduce the heat to low, and simmer until the

recipe continues on page 131 »

Chicken Potpie

continued

mixture thickens, about 10 minutes. Stir in the chicken, peas, corn, parsley, salt, and pepper. Taste and adjust the seasoning. Transfer the mixture to a pie dish 9 inches in diameter and 1 to 1½ inches deep.

On a lightly floured surface, roll out the dough to a 12-inch-diameter round. Trim the edges, then brush some of the egg yolk mixture around the edge of the round. Place the dough, egg side down, on top of the filling. Trim off any excess dough and push the dough firmly against the rim of the dish so it forms a seal. (If not, you risk it bubbling over.) Brush the surface of the pie dough with more of the egg yolk mixture. Cut a slit in the center of the dough to allow steam to escape.

Place on a baking sheet and bake until the crust is golden brown, 35 to 40 minutes. Serve immediately.

List *of* Ingredients

Crust: 1½ cups all-purpose flour · ¼ cup shredded Cheddar cheese · 1½ tablespoons minced fresh rosemary · Pinch of salt · 6 tablespoons cold unsalted butter, cut into small pieces · 2 tablespoons cold vegetable shortening · ⅓ cup whole milk

Filling: 4 tablespoons unsalted butter · 3 carrots, chopped · 1 large baking potato, peeled and diced · 2 leeks, rinsed and sliced · ¼ cup all-purpose flour · 1 cup chicken broth · ½ cup dry white wine · 1 cup half-and-half · 3 cups cubed cooked chicken (about 3 boneless, skinless chicken breast halves) · 1 cup fresh or thawed frozen peas · 1 cup fresh or thawed frozen corn kernels · ¼ cup chopped minced fresh flat-leaf (Italian) parsley · 2 teaspoons salt · ½ teaspoon freshly ground pepper

1 egg yolk beaten with 1 teaspoon water

Velvet Birthday Cake
with Vanilla Buttercream Frosting

MAKES ONE 9-INCH 2-LAYER CAKE; SERVES TEN TO TWELVE

It's said the world is divided between chocolate-lovers and lemon-lovers. This is all well and good in the ordinary dessert world, but can pose a problem when it comes to choosing a birthday cake flavor. Let's face it, you have only a 50 percent chance of success. This is why I opt for the simplicity and elegance of the old-fashioned, velvety 1-2-3-4 yellow cake (1 cup butter, 2 cups sugar, 3 cups flour, 4 eggs) with a rich vanilla buttercream frosting. Personalize the cake decoration in honor of the birthday boy or girl and enjoy the sweet satisfaction that comes from making a cake from scratch.

Brush two 9-inch round cake pans with the 2 tablespoons melted butter and dust with flour, tapping out the excess flour. Preheat the oven to 350°F.

In a medium bowl, whisk the flour, baking powder, and salt together. Set aside.

In a large bowl, using an electric mixer on medium-high speed, beat the 1 cup butter until soft. Add the sugar and beat until smooth and fluffy. Add the vanilla extract and beat until incorporated. Add the eggs, one at a time, beating well after each addition. As you beat the eggs, pause several times to scrape down the sides of the bowl.

recipe continues on next page »

133

Velvet Birthday Cake *with* Vanilla Buttercream Frosting

continued

With the mixer on low speed, alternately add the flour mixture and milk, beginning and ending with the flour mixture. Divide the batter between the pans and spread it evenly. Bake until a skewer inserted into the center of a cake layer comes out clean and the tops are lightly springy to the touch, about 30 minutes. Let the layers cool in their pans on a wire rack for 10 to 15 minutes. Run a knife around the edges of the pan and turn out the layers. Let cool completely before frosting.

To frost the layers, put one layer, top side down, on a serving plate. Using a frosting spatula or knife, spread the layer with about one-third of the buttercream, adding more on the top than on the sides. Invert the other layer, top side down, on the first layer. Spread the remaining buttercream on the top and sides of the cake. If the buttercream becomes too soft, refrigerate for 10 to 15 minutes and then continue. Refrigerate the cake for at least 30 minutes to allow the frosting to set.

List *of* Ingredients

2 tablespoons unsalted butter, melted, plus 1 cup (2 sticks) unsalted butter at room temperature · 3 cups all-purpose flour, plus more for dusting · 1 tablespoon baking powder · ½ teaspoon salt · 2 cups granulated sugar · 1 teaspoon vanilla extract · 4 eggs · 1 cup whole milk · Vanilla Buttercream Frosting (page 135)

Vanilla Buttercream Frosting

MAKES THREE CUPS, ENOUGH FOR A 9-INCH
2-LAYER CAKE

The quintessential birthday cake frosting, this buttercream is the epitome of sinful indulgence. Forget the cake. Give me buttercream! You will need an instant-read thermometer for this recipe. If you don't already own one, you should, as it comes in handy for a variety of cooking tasks.

In a medium bowl, using an electric mixer set on medium speed, beat the butter until it is very soft and creamy. Set aside.

In a small saucepan, combine the milk, cream, and ⅓ cup of the sugar. Cook over medium heat, stirring occasionally, until bubbles appear around the edges of the pan.

In a medium bowl, combine the egg yolks and the remaining ⅓ cup sugar and beat on medium speed until thick and pale, about 3 minutes. Reduce the mixer speed to low and, with the mixer running, gradually pour in the hot milk mixture. Return the mixture to the saucepan.

Cook the mixture over medium heat, whisking constantly, until it registers 165°F on an instant-read thermometer, about 5 minutes. Pour the mixture back into a large bowl and let cool for 10 minutes. Beat in the vanilla. Add the butter in 3 increments, beating each addition until completely blended before adding the next.

Use the buttercream frosting immediately or refrigerate until needed. If you do refrigerate it for any length of time (you can do so for up to 3 days), you will need to whisk it over simmering water until it reaches a spreadable consistency again.

List *of* Ingredients

1½ cups (3 sticks) unsalted butter at room temperature ·
6 tablespoons whole millk · 2 tablespoons heavy cream · ⅔ cup sugar · 5 egg yolks ·
2 teaspoons vanilla extract

winter sensations

CATCH a snowflake on your tongue, TRIM a tree,

DECORATE cookies, SIP hot cocoa, HEAR a chorus sing,

MAKE snow angels, WARM your toes by the fire, REFLECT on the year,

REVEL in the fragrance of balsam or pine or bay, GET rosy cheeks,

FORCE an amaryllis bulb, BELIEVE,

enjoy a winter holiday with your senses every invigorating day.

WINTER CELEBRATIONS

Under a blanket of quiet, winter tucks us indoors. This season of
warming sips and quiet light prompts us to explore our inner lives. What matters
most to us within these sheltering walls—and within ourselves?

Nature, in the midst of deep chill, even now ignites our senses. Against a neutral canvas of snow or leafless trees, we see black-capped chickadees interspersed with scarlet cardinals and blue-sheened jays. We sleep under the halo of a million shimmering stars. We hear dripping icicles and creaking birch trunks. We smell frost and wet mittens. We feel our cheeks turning red outside and our cold fingers thawing as we grasp warm mugs of cocoa inside. We taste candied nuts and spicy peppermint, earthy cheeses and sunny citrus.

Balance the chill outside with heady scents and warm hues inside. Trim a rosemary topiary with tiny silver bulbs for the holidays, then remove the bulbs (or not) and enjoy the beauty and aroma of the rosemary through January and February and beyond. Fashion clove-studded pomanders from tangerines, oranges, and lemons. Their spicy, sunny scents will surprise passersby. Capture holiday memories in a photo display tray. Make an indoor cactus garden for the New Year. It will transport you to warmer climes.

Celebrate with a cozy Sunday supper of cassoulet, a classic French peasant dish of lamb, pork, and beans. As the cassoulet bubbles in the oven, an aromatic conjuring occurs. Burdens melt away and the psyche lightens up. Enjoy a sip of red wine. Or opt for an amusing Charades and Chardonnay party (page 151) that incorporates an easy-to-prepare hors d'oeuvre buffet. It proves that long winter nights were designed for enjoyment. If you don't know, or have forgotten, how to play Charades, help is at hand! I have included the how-to's in this section (page 162). Give it a try. You're guaranteed a laugh.

What will bring you pleasure inside when the world is (seemingly) sleeping outside? Firelight warms the body as well as the soul, plus it gives us a rosy glow. Candlelight brings about the same effect on a more diminutive scale. Why not fashion a candlescape in your fireplace? Arrange various sizes of pillar candles in an empty fireplace, choosing candles scented with pine or cinnamon, and add pinecones and curly willow or birch branches for accents. Settle into a cozy chair and meditate on the flames.

In the chill of winter, warm the heart of someone you love with a scented love letter. Pen your words (let them know how you really feel!) and then slip fragrant herbs or rose petals into the envelope. Mail the letter to someone far away (or one street over), place it on a child's pillow, or tuck it into your lover's briefcase.

The kitchen is an ideal place to reflect on love and life. Think of cooking as a moving meditation. The rhythm of chopping vegetables, the sound of onions sautéing, and the mélange of aromas can put us in harmony with the world, even when the weather is cold and gray. Take advantage of these long nights to cook for those you love and to truly celebrate the season.

We tend to think about others during this month of holidays and celebrations, but why not make giving a monthly ritual? It doesn't take much time to drop off a plant at a nursing home (ask a nurse to give it to someone who doesn't receive much) or to clean out a drawer and assemble a bag for Goodwill. If you're a baker, why not bake an extra batch of cookies and give them to a neighbor? Get your kids involved, too. When you sow the giving seed, you cultivate gratitude.

This section will inspire you to celebrate the frosty season with heartfelt warmth. When you give and receive, toast and trim, may you do so with childlike enthusiasm and glee.

Project *No.* One

CACTUS GARDEN

When you gaze out the window on a gray winter day, wouldn't it be nice to be reminded of someplace sunny and warm? Plant cacti in small pots or shallow bowls. Cover with small stones or rough sand. Place on the windowsill. Instant desert!

Project *No.* Two

SCENTED LOVE LETTER

Why not write one to somebody you love? When you do, slip a bouquet of fragrant herbs, such as lavender, thyme, and rosemary, tied with narrow ribbon, into the envelope, too. Rose petals are also delightful.

Project *No.* Three

POMANDERS

Stud oranges and other citrus with whole cloves to make aromatic pomanders. Hang them from doorknobs or pile them in graduated mixing bowls for a tiered centerpiece.

George,

Project *No.* Five

FIREPLACE CANDLESCAPE

Arrange various sizes of pillar candles in an empty fireplace. Accent with pinecones and curly willow or birch branches. Choose candles scented with pine or cinnamon for seasonal fragrance.

Project *No.* Six

Project *No.* Four

BEJEWELED STARS

Spend some quality family time making bejeweled star ornaments: Bend thin wire into a star shape, then string tiny beads or pearls onto it and close by twisting the ends together. Attach the star to a gift or hang as a window or tree ornament.

GLITTERY CELLOPHANE FAVORS

Chocolates or glacéed fruits wrapped in cellophane make sweet party favors or stocking stuffers. Tie the cellophane with pretty ribbon and add a glass jewel or millinery ornament.

Project *No.* Seven

TWINE CANDLEHOLDERS

Utilitarian as twine may be, it's quite interesting to look at, too. Collect balls of twine in various sizes and insert dripless candles in the hole in the center of each. Group together on your dining table or line up along your fireplace mantel.

Project *No.* Eight

PHOTO DISPLAY TRAY

Winter brings many occasions for photos, as well as another New Year's resolution to organize and display them. I'll leave the organization to you. Here's an idea for display: Make a photo tray. Look for an old tea tray with a glass insert, or a framed print whose value to you is in the frame. Arrange photos under the glass. The tray will serve up conversation as well as food and drinks.

Project *No.* Nine

ALTERNATIVE CHRISTMAS TREE

Plant a large rosemary topiary in a galvanized aluminum
bucket or a red ceramic pot. Decorate with tiny silver
ornaments and little white lights.

Project *No.* Ten

PLANTER CITRUS TREE

Potted citrus lends beauty and fragrance to a sunny room or porch. In
the gray days of winter, when citrus is at its peak, a small dwarf tangerine
or Meyer lemon tree will make you happy. When you entertain, you can
transform the tree into a buffet or table decoration. It looks nice with little
white lights strung on it, too. Look for dwarf-citrus growers online, or visit
your local nursery.

Plant your citrus tree in a pot that is at least 8 inches wider and deeper
than the tree's root ball. The pot should have a drainage hole. Before you
insert the plant into the pot, place terra-cotta shards (a good use of a broken flowerpot) in the bottom of the pot and fill it about one-fourth full
with soil mix. Remove the tree from its plastic, gently coax out the roots,
and place it in the pot. Fill the pot with soil mix. Place the tree in a sunny
spot and water well about twice a week. Fertilize with a fertilizer recom-
mended for citrus, according to package directions.

Project *No.* Eleven

SIT AND SIP: HOT TODDY

There's a lot to think about during the winter, from creating holiday gift lists to musing about when, in heaven's name, the sleet will stop. Now's the time for a hot toddy.

To make one: Fill a mug or glass three-quarters full with hot tea. Stir in 1 tablespoon honey and 2 shots brandy. Add a lemon slice and a clove or two. Sip and savor.

Project *No.* Twelve

HOSTESS (AND HOST) FLOWERS

Plant seasonal bulbs such as paper whites or amaryllis in beautiful bowls or clear glass hurricane candle holders and give them to friends who are hosting a party. Once the bulbs have flowered and faded, the vessels will remain for enjoyment. You might even see them in use at the next party.

CHARADES AND CHARDONNAY

MENU

Sliced Smoked Duck *or* Turkey *with your* Favorite Chutney

Deviled Crab Dip

Honest *and* Good Onion Dip

Curried Parsnip Soup Sips

Serrano Ham *and* Cider Blue Cheese Crostini

Sweet *and* Spicy Nut Brittle

This is a grown-up party that my friends and I have been enjoying for years.
If you're a working mom like me, and continuously struggle
with the guilt that comes from not spending every waking moment with your
precious ones, let me absolve you of it straightaway.

An evening with good friends, fueled by good food, a smooth sip, and a competitive game of charades, will recharge your spirit and sense of humor. You'll also feel as if you've been time-warped back to an era gone by, when TV and DVD were merely letters and parlor games were the evening entertainment.

This is an everyday celebration that lends itself to indoor or outdoor entertaining, but it's particularly nice indoors on a chilly evening, especially if you have a crackling fire in the fireplace. Since this get-together is literally a movable feast, with people charading and eating at different times, a buffet is the way to go. It frees you up for full-out participation and enables guests to serve themselves between sets.

The hors d'oeuvre menu offers make-ahead ease, colorful presentation, and flexibility. You can prepare the entire menu or make only one or two recipes and purchase the rest, such as the smoked duck or turkey along with the chutney. Why not take advantage of the talents of other cooks?

The Charades and Chardonnay party detailed here has a wine-country aesthetic. Richly hued artisanal pottery and linens set a stunning stage for this fun and flavorsome celebration. Wine bottles are tucked into ice-packed terra-cotta planters, and nuts and popcorn are placed on an old wine barrel top that's been converted into a lazy Susan. Serving pieces in various heights, colors, and textures give visual interest to the display. Potted dwarf citrus trees that normally reside in my kitchen do double duty as decoration for the table. It's a presentation that is at once relaxed and elegant.

Deviled Crab Dip

This richly satisfying, warm dip has a spicy bite, hence the description "deviled."
A friend of mine calls it "a never-ending crab cake."

Preheat the oven to 375°F. Butter a 6-cup baking dish.

In a medium skillet or sauté pan, melt the 2 tablespoons butter over low heat. Add the onion and cook until softened, about 3 minutes. Add the bell pepper and celery and cook, stirring, for 2 minutes more. Remove from the heat.

Put 2 cups of the bread crumbs in a large bowl and gradually stir the milk into the crumbs. Mix well. Let stand for 5 minutes, stirring occasionally to make sure the crumbs are moistened evenly. Add the crabmeat, onion mixture, parsley, lemon juice, and dry mustard. Mix well. Add the cayenne, and salt and black pepper.

Spoon the mixture into the baking dish. Place the remaining bread crumbs in a bowl and stir the melted butter into the crumbs. Toss the bread crumbs to coat with the butter. Sprinkle evenly over the crab mixture.

Bake until lightly browned, 25 to 30 minutes. Serve with the crudités or crackers.

List *of* Ingredients

2 tablespoons unsalted butter, plus 3 tablespoons unsalted butter, melted ·
1 large yellow onion, finely chopped · 1 green bell pepper, seeded, deribbed, and finely chopped ·
3 stalks celery, finely chopped · 3 cups fresh bread crumbs · ½ cup whole milk ·
1 pound fresh lump crabmeat, picked over for shell · ½ cup minced fresh flat-leaf (Italian) parsley ·
2 tablespoons fresh lemon juice · 1 teaspoon dry mustard · ⅛ teaspoon cayenne pepper ·
Salt and freshly ground black pepper to taste · Crudités or crackers for serving

Honest *and* Good Onion Dip

MAKES ABOUT ONE CUP

This onion dip is "honest" because it's homemade
and "good" because it's downright delish. Its sweet, caramelized flavor and
sinfully creamy texture make this dip irresistible. If you have the time,
refrigerate it overnight and the flavors will sing even more harmoniously.
Serve with potato chips, crackers, or vegetables.

In a medium sauté pan, melt the butter with the olive oil over medium-high heat. Add the onions and sauté until translucent, about 3 minutes. Reduce the heat to low and cook, stirring occasionally, until the onions are very soft and golden brown, 15 to 20 minutes. Transfer the onions to a bowl and let cool.

In a medium bowl, combine the sour cream, mayonnaise, and lemon juice. Add the onions and mix well. Season with salt and pepper and hot sauce.

List *of* Ingredients

2 tablespoons unsalted butter • 2 tablespoons olive oil • 2 yellow onions, coarsely chopped • ½ cup sour cream • ½ cup mayonnaise • ½ teaspoon fresh lemon juice • Salt and freshly ground pepper to taste • Dash of hot sauce

Curried Parsnip Soup Sips

SERVES EIGHT IN SMALL CUPS

Parsnips make a wonderful and healthful base for soups.
Like potatoes, they contribute a satisfying texture, and their subtle spiciness
marries fabulously with curry. You'll love the happy golden color, too.
If you have the time, fry a few thin slices of parsnip in olive oil and use as a garnish.
For an easy—and pretty—presentation, serve the soup in demitasse cups
so your guests can sip rather than fuss with spoons.

In a large, deep saucepan, melt the butter over medium-high heat. Add the parsnips, onion, and potato and sauté for 5 minutes. Stir in the curry powder. Reduce the heat to low, add the chicken broth, and simmer until the vegetables are tender, about 20 minutes.

Transfer to a blender or food processor and blend until smooth (you may have to do this in batches). Return the soup to the saucepan and place over medium-high heat. Add the dry mustard, turmeric, and salt and pepper. Bring to a boil, then reduce heat and simmer until heated through.

List *of* Ingredients

2 tablespoons unsalted butter · 3 parsnips, peeled and coarsely chopped ·
1 yellow onion, coarsely chopped · 1 baking potato, peeled and coarsely chopped ·
1 tablespoon plus 1 teaspoon curry powder · 5 cups chicken broth · 1 teaspoon dry mustard ·
½ teaspoon ground turmeric · Salt and freshly ground pepper to taste

Serrano Ham *and* Cider Blue Cheese Crostini

MAKES ABOUT THIRTY CROSTINI

When I lived in Madrid, I spent many Sunday evenings in a small bar on the Plaza Mayor that served hard cider and this tapa. Cabrales is a robust blue cheese from northern Spain, and serrano ham is similar to, yet earthier than, Italian prosciutto. Indeed, if you can't find serrano ham, opt for prosciutto.

Preheat the broiler. In a small bowl, combine the blue cheese, cream cheese, ¼ cup apple cider, and lemon juice. Using a fork, mix and mash until a spreadable paste forms, adding more cider if necessary.

Cut the bread into ¼-inch-thick diagonal slices and arrange on a baking sheet. Place under the broiler and toast until golden. Lightly brush the toasts on one side with the olive oil.

Spread the cheese mixture on the olive oil–side of the toasts. Cut each slice of ham in half lengthwise. Roll the slices into spirals and place 1 on each of the toasts.

List *of* Ingredients

½ cup (4 ounces) blue cheese, such as Cabrales, Gorgonzola, or Roquefort, at room temperature • ½ cup (4 ounces) cream cheese at room temperature • ¼ cup hard apple cider, plus more as needed • 1 teaspoon fresh lemon juice • 1 sweet baguette • ¼ cup extra-virgin olive oil • 15 thin slices (about 6 ounces) serrano ham or prosciutto

Sweet *and* Spicy Nut Brittle

MAKES ABOUT TWO CUPS

This nibble not only tastes great but the brittlelike shards are
dramatic looking, too. You can make this spicy-sweet treat with one nut variety
(I like to use macadamia nuts) or mix 'em up. Go nuts!

Line a baking sheet with parchment paper. In a large bowl, combine the
salt, cumin, ginger, coriander, cayenne, and the 1 tablespoon sugar. Stir to
blend. Set aside.

In a large, heavy skillet or sauté pan, heat the oil over medium-high
heat. Add the nuts and sprinkle the ½ cup of sugar over them. Cook the
nuts, tossing constantly, until they are golden and the sugar has caramelized, 3 to 5 minutes, depending on the nut variety. Adjust the heat as necessary to prevent the nuts from burning.

Scrape the nut mixture into the bowl with the spice mixture and toss
quickly to coat the nuts with the spices. Pour the mixture onto the prepared baking sheet, separating any nuts that stick together. Let the brittle
cool and set, about 15 minutes. The oil may separate from the nuts as they
cool. This is fine. Once they cool, break the brittle into shards.

List *of* Ingredients

1½ teaspoons salt · 1½ teaspoons ground cumin · ½ teaspoon ground ginger ·
½ teaspoon ground coriander · Pinch of cayenne pepper · 1 tablespoon sugar, plus ½ cup ·
¼ cup canola oil · 8 ounces (about 2 cups) unsalted nuts of your choice

How *to* Play Charades

Charades is a game of pantomime. One person acts out a word or phrase without speaking, while the other team members guess what the word or phrase is. The objective is for the guessers to figure out the word or phrase as quickly as possible. You'll laugh yourself silly. It's good fun.

EQUIPMENT

A stopwatch or other timer · A notepad and pencil for scorekeeping · Blank slips of paper · Two baskets or other containers for the slips

PREGAME PREPARATION

Choose your teams. Each team should have the same number of members, if possible. Give each team blank slips of paper. Select a timekeeper/scorekeeper from each team. Determine the number of rounds you'll play. Make sure everybody knows the hand signals (see facing page).

The teams convene in separate rooms to come up with phrases to put on their pieces of paper. These phrases may be quotations or titles of books, movies, plays, television shows, and/or songs.

TIME TO PLAY

Each round of the game proceeds as follows:

A player from Team A draws a phrase slip from Team B's basket and is allowed a few moments to review the slip. The timekeeper for Team B notes the time and tells the player to start. Team A then has 3 minutes to guess the phrase. If they guess it, the timekeeper notes how long it took for the team to guess correctly. If they do not guess it in 3 minutes, the timekeeper calls time, and records a time of 3 minutes.

A player from Team B draws a phrase slip from Team A's basket, and play continues as above, with Team A's timekeeper watching the clock. The game proceeds until every player has had a chance to "act." The scorekeepers tally the scores, and the team with the smallest score (the least amount of time to guess phrases) wins.

HAND SIGNALS

At no time may a word be uttered or mouthed in charades. To act out a phrase, a player begins by indicating what category the phrase is in, and how many words are in the phrase. The words in the phrase are acted out one at a time, although they can be acted out in any order the player chooses. Alternatively, the player may act out the complete concept of the phrase at once.

CATEGORIES

BOOK TITLE: Unfold your hands as if they were a book opening.

MOVIE TITLE: Crank an old-fashioned movie camera.

PLAY TITLE: Pull the rope that opens a theater curtain.

SONG TITLE: Pretend to sing.

TV SHOW: Draw a rectangle to outline a TV screen.

QUOTE OR PHRASE: Make quotation marks in the air with your fingers.

OTHER INFORMATION

NUMBER OF WORDS IN THE TITLE: Hold up the number of fingers.

WHICH WORD YOU'RE WORKING ON: Hold up the number of fingers.

NUMBER OF SYLLABLES IN THE WORD: Lay the number of fingers on your arm.

WHICH SYLLABLE YOU'RE WORKING ON: Lay the number of fingers on your arm.

LENGTH OF WORD: Make a "little" or "big" sign as if you were measuring a fish.

"THE WHOLE CONCEPT": Sweep your arms through the air.

"YOUR GUESS IS CORRECT": Touch your nose with a finger of one hand, while pointing at the person with your other hand.

"SOUNDS LIKE": Cup one hand behind an ear.

"LONGER VERSION OF": Pretend to stretch a piece of elastic, for example, to lengthen a guess of "paper" to "newspaper."

"SHORTER VERSION OF": Do a "karate chop" with your hand, for example, to shorten a guess of "sewing" to "sew."

"PLURAL": Link your little fingers.

"PAST TENSE": Wave your hand over your shoulder toward your back.

"A LETTER OF THE ALPHABET": Move your hand in a chopping motion toward your arm (near the top of your forearm if the letter is near the beginning of the alphabet, or near the bottom of your arm if the letter is near the end of the alphabet).

"YOU'RE ON THE WRONG TRACK": Wave your hands, palms down, over one another as if declaring "safe on base."

"YOU'RE ON THE RIGHT TRACK": Wave your hands toward yourself.

SUNDAY DINNER

MENU

Winter Salad *with* Roquefort *and* Pears

Petit Cassoulet

Pink Grapefruit Shortcake

For some, indulgence is a hot fudge sundae or a new pair of shoes.
For me, it's a long, lazy Sunday afternoon at home, the kitchen filled with the
cozy aroma of supper cooking in the oven.

When I was a child, my mother would rise early to begin preparing the roast we would enjoy for Sunday dinner, a meal that occurred not at the normal dinner (or what was then called supper) hour of 6 P.M. but at 2 P.M. Does such a thing still exist, I wonder? Into the oven the roast would go, and off we would go to church. On returning, we entered a house redolent with the cheering aroma of roast pork or lamb or beef, depending on the season. To give this same gift to my own family, I do so with a slow-cooked dish such as the Petit Cassoulet in this menu.

This classic dish from France offers a wealth of flavors, including lamb, pork shoulder, sausage, and white beans, crowned with crunchy golden bread crumbs. I call mine a petit cassoulet because my recipe is a simplified version of the original, though it deliv-ers the same wonderful tastes and textures. You can begin cooking the cassoulet in the morning and finish it in the late afternoon, when it will emerge from the oven, hot and bubbling, just in time for supper. A salad of winter greens with Roquefort and pears balances the headiness of the cassoulet. Pink Grapefruit Shortcake concludes the meal with its sunny sweet-tart flavor.

The rustic elegance of this menu calls for a table that is equally so. Here, it is set minimally with black-and-white bistro plates on a natural cotton tablecloth for a warm and restful effect. In the center of the table, tropical fruits are casually arranged in a compote dish, their colors and scents evoking warm climes. Beeswax candles on pewter saucers wink gently as we revisit our weekend and make plans for the coming week.

Winter Salad *with* Roquefort *and* Pears

SERVES EIGHT AS A SIDE DISH

Crisp textures and full flavors make this a salad that can stand up to the richness of cassoulet. It's terrific with roast meats and poultry, too.

In the bottom of a large salad bowl, stir the red wine vinegar, mustard, and salt and pepper together. Gradually whisk in the walnut oil. Add the cheese and stir to combine.

Add the lettuce, pears, red onion, and bell pepper to the bowl. Just before serving, toss gently to coat with the dressing. Sprinkle with the nuts and serve.

List *of* Ingredients

6 tablespoons red wine vinegar ·
2 teaspoons Dijon mustard · Salt and freshly ground pepper to taste · 1 cup walnut oil ·
¼ cup crumbled Roquefort or other blue cheese · Leaves from 2 small heads romaine lettuce, torn into
bite-sized pieces · 3 ripe but firm pears, such as Bosc or Red Crimson, halved, cored, and
thinly sliced · 1 small red onion, thinly sliced · 1 red bell pepper, seeded, deribbed, and thinly sliced ·
¼ cup coarsely chopped walnuts

Petit Cassoulet

SERVES EIGHT TO TEN AS A MAIN COURSE

This classic French peasant dish is one of the most savory and satisfying
meals I know. It makes a memorable meal for family suppers as
well as for entertaining. You can make the cassoulet up to 2 days in advance.
This is a casual dish; serve it directly from the pot.

Put the beans in a large Dutch oven or casserole and fill the pot two-thirds
full with water. Place over high heat and bring to a boil. Tie the bay leaf,
cloves, and thyme in a cheesecloth bag (or put them in a tea ball) and add
to the beans along with the onion. Reduce the heat and simmer the beans,
stirring occasionally, until tender, about 1 hour. If the water gets too low as
the beans simmer, add more water. You will need 4 cups of bean broth.
Drain, reserving the liquid and beans separately and discarding the herbs
and onion. Remove any beans that have stuck to the bottom of the pot.

Preheat the oven to 350°F. Heat the same Dutch oven or casserole
over low heat, add the bacon, and fry until it begins to brown, about
5 minutes. Using a slotted spoon, remove the bacon and save for another
use. Reserve the drippings.

Generously season the lamb and pork with salt and pepper to taste
and add to the pot with the sausage. Place in the oven and roast, turning

recipe continues on page 172 »

Petit Cassoulet

continued

occasionally, until the meats are well browned and tender, about 1¼ hours. Remove from the oven and let the meats cool. Cut the meats into 1½-inch pieces. Drain the pot, reserving ½ cup of the drippings.

Place one-third of the drained beans in the same pot. Arrange half the meats on top of the beans, along with 3 of the garlic cloves. Add one-third of the remaining beans, then the rest of the meats and the 3 remaining garlic cloves. Top with the remaining beans and sprinkle with salt and pepper to taste.

In a bowl, whisk together the tomato paste and ground thyme, along with the 1 teaspoon salt, the ½ teaspoon pepper, and 3 cups of the reserved bean broth. Drizzle the reserved drippings and 2½ to 3 cups of this mixture into the pot. The beans should look well coated with liquid but should not be floating. Bake, uncovered, for 1 hour, adding more bean broth to the mixture if needed to prevent the beans from drying out. In a bowl, mix the bread crumbs and the parsley. Sprinkle the bread crumbs over the cassoulet and continue to bake until the beans are tender and the bread crumb mixture is golden, about 1 hour longer.

List *of* Ingredients

3 cups dried Great Northern beans • 1 bay leaf • 4 whole cloves •
4 thyme sprigs • 1 yellow onion, cut in half • 1 pound slab bacon or salt pork, finely chopped •
2 pounds boneless leg of lamb, in 2 pieces • 2 pounds pork shoulder, in 2 pieces •
Salt to taste, plus 1 teaspoon • Freshly ground pepper to taste, plus ½ teaspoon • 1 pound mild Italian sausage •
6 garlic cloves, crushed • 3 tablespoons tomato paste • 1 teaspoon ground thyme •
1½ cups dried bread crumbs • 1 cup minced fresh flat-leaf (Italian) parsley

Pink Grapefruit Shortcake

SERVES EIGHT AS A DESSERT

Don't relegate shortcake to warm-weather dining.
It's delectable when made with winter fruits, too. Pink grapefruit, with its
sunny flavor, low acidity, and luminous color, is a wonderful complement
to the rich shortcake laced with crystallized ginger.

Preheat the oven to 400°F. In a small bowl, combine the grapefruit sections and the ½ cup sugar. Stir gently and let stand at room temperature for 1 hour.

In a food processor, combine the flour, the 2 tablespoons sugar, the baking powder, and salt. Pulse once or twice to combine. Add the butter and candied ginger and process just until the mixture resembles rolled oats. Transfer the mixture to a medium bowl. Using a fork, gradually stir in the milk until the mixture forms a soft dough.

recipe continues on page 175»

Pink Grapefruit Shortcake

continued

On a lightly floured board, pat the dough out to a ½-inch thickness. Using a 3-inch round cookie cutter, cut into rounds. Transfer to an ungreased baking sheet and bake until golden brown, about 15 minutes.

In a deep bowl, beat the heavy cream with the confectioners' sugar until soft peaks form. To serve, split the shortcakes and spoon sweetened grapefruit onto the bottom cake. Top with whipped cream and more fruit. Replace the top of the shortcake. Serve warm or at room temperature.

Note on Peeling and Segmenting Grapefruit: Using a sharp knife, cut off the very top and bottom of the grapefruit. Place the fruit on a cutting board and cut the rind and pith from the flesh, starting at the top and following the curves down. Hold the grapefruit over a bowl and, using a paring knife, cut out each section of the fruit by inserting the blade of the knife between the flesh and the membrane on both sides.

List *of* Ingredients

3 large pink grapefruit, such as Ruby Red or Rio Star, peeled, segmented, and drained well (see note) •
½ cup granulated sugar, plus 2 tablespoons • 2 cups all-purpose flour • 1 tablespoon baking powder • 1 teaspoon salt •
4 tablespoons cold unsalted butter, cut into 4 pieces • ¼ cup minced candied ginger • ⅔ cup whole milk •
1¼ cups heavy cream • 2 tablespoons confectioners' sugar

Acknowledgments

MILLE GRAZIE

❧

A book is a labor of love on the part of many.
I'd like to thank them.

France Ruffenach, thank you for photographs teeming with beauty and spirit (just like you). Aaron Hom, my flawless stylist, rides the same aesthetic wave as I do. Thanks for bringing to life my ideas in such "gorzchwa" fashion. Pouke made the food look stellar with seemingly little effort and much grace. Jeff Larsen, thanks for your quiet, sweet presence and your wonderful work. Amanda Haas, who tested all the recipes for me, brought enthusiasm and insight to the project. Reyn thanks you all, too.

I am grateful to the fabulous people at Chronicle Books. Thanks to my wonderful editor, Leslie Jonath, who shepherded this book with enthusiasm and attention. Kevin Toyama, I appreciate your organizational skills (thank heavens!). Carolyn Miller, my copy editor, finessed my writing and I am a better writer for it. Sara Schneider wrapped beautiful book design around my words (and she knits, too!). Thanks to Beth Steiner for overseeing the production elements. Last but not least, I'm grateful to Angela Miller, my literary agent, who got the whole thing started.

So many people encourage and support me in my work. Among them, Bill Stankey and Mary Lalli at Westport Entertainment Associates; all the folks at NBC's *Today* show, including Dee Dee Thomas, Betsy Alexander, Katie, Matt, Ann, and Al; Nancy Kay; Tori Ritchie; Mary Ann Barr; and Gates McKibbin.

And then there are the near and dear who make me laugh and love me, too: Amanda and Jeff Marcus, Kathryn Kleinman and Michael Schwab, Sue and Peter Chase, and my wild, wacky family (on both sides). And, of course, the nearest and dearest (and the most patient, too), my husband, Courtney Reeser, who weathers photo shoots in our home, tolerates props in every nook and cranny, supports my travel schedule and deadline demands, and still manages to encourage and contribute with enthusiasm. Courtney's spirit and his sense of style enrich my life every day, and thus they enhance this book, too.

INDEX

A

Alternative Christmas Tree, 147
Apples
    Cinnamon Applesauce, 101
    Dried Apples and Pears, 105
    Three-Apple Crisp, 121
Arugula, Cherry Tomato, and Prosciutto
    Salad, 29
Asparagus and Basil Frittata, 30
Autumn Minestrone with Tiny
    Turkey Meatballs, 113–14
Autumn Salad with Persimmons
    and Pecans, 111

B

Basque Bell Pepper and Tomato Salad, 83
Beach-Pebble Drainer, 62
Beans
    Autumn Minestrone with Tiny Turkey
        Meatballs, 113–114
    Paella a la Valenciana, 84–86
    Petit Cassoulet, 170–72
    Smoky Green Beans, 48
Beets, Roasted, with Blue Cheese
    and Walnuts, 127
Bejeweled Stars, 143
Bell peppers
    Basque Bell Pepper and Tomato Salad, 83
    roasting and peeling, 83
Berries. *See also individual berries*
    Midsummer's Eve Syllabub, 57
Beverages
    Blueberry Limeade, 62
    Blushing Sangria, 90
    Cardamom Coffee, 97
    Hot Toddy, 148
    Limoncello, 22
    Root Beer Floats, 62
Bird in the Grass Centerpiece, 17
Birthday Cake, Velvet, with Vanilla
    Buttercream Frosting, 133–35
Black Pepper Cream, 120
Blanket Bliss, 102

Blueberries
    Blueberry Limeade, 62
    Blueberry Turkey Sausage Patties, 70
    Cherry-Blueberry Compote with
        Brown Sugar Mascarpone, 75
    Nectarine-Ginger Pancakes with
        World's Easiest Blueberry Sauce, 68
    Old-Fashioned Blueberry Muffins
        with Streusel Topping, 71–72
Blushing Sangria, 90
Bread
    Serrano Ham and Cider Blue Cheese
        Crostini, 158
    Wild Mushroom Topping for
        Crusty Bread, 112
Buttermilk-Herb Dressing, 34

C

Cactus Garden, 140
Cake, Velvet Birthday, with Vanilla
    Buttercream Frosting, 133–35
Cake-Stand Condiment Server, 19
Candles
    Climbing Votives, 58
    Fireplace Candlescape, 143
    Fresh Flower Votives, 20
    Moss Candlescape, 98
    Twine Candleholders, 144
Cape Cod Clam Chowder, 116–17
Cardamom Coffee, 97
Cassoulet, Petit, 170–72
Centerpiece, Bird in the Grass, 17
Charades, 162–63
Cheese
    Cherry-Blueberry Compote
        with Brown Sugar Mascarpone, 75
    Roasted Beets with Blue Cheese
        and Walnuts, 127
    Serrano Ham and Cider Blue Cheese
        Crostini, 158
    Winter Salad with Roquefort and
        Pears, 169
Cherries
    Autumn Salad with Persimmons and
        Pecans, 111

Cherry-Blueberry Compote
    with Brown Sugar Mascarpone, 75
Cherry Tomato, Arugula, and
    Prosciutto Salad, 29
Chestnut Soup with Black Pepper Cream,
    119–20
Chicken
    Chicken Croquettes with Buttermilk-
        Herb Dressing, 33–34
    Chicken Potpie, 129–31
    Paella a la Valenciana, 84–86
    Roast Chicken with Asian Flavors, 44
Chowder, Cape Cod Clam, 116–17
Christmas Tree, Alternative, 147
Chutney, Rhubarb, 19
Cinnamon Applesauce, 101
Citrus Tree, Planter, 147
Clams
    Cape Cod Clam Chowder, 116–17
    Paella a la Valenciana, 84–86
Climbing Votives, 58
Coconut Rice, 47
Coffee, Cardamom, 97
Condiment Server, Cake-Stand, 19
Cookies, Spanish Sugar, 87
Copper Foil Oak Leaves, 98
Crab Dip, Deviled, 155
Crisp, Three-Apple, 121
Crostini, Serrano Ham and
    Cider Blue Cheese, 158
Crystallized Flowers, 14
Cucumber Salad, Refreshing, 46
Cupcake Greetings, 14
Curried Parsnip Soup Sips, 157

D

Desserts
    Cherry-Blueberry Compote with Brown
        Sugar Mascarpone, 75
    Cupcake Greetings, 14
    Lemon and Orange Sorbets in Citrus
        Cups, 89
    Midsummer's Eve Syllabub, 57
    Pink Grapefruit Shortcake, 173–75
    Root Beer Floats, 62
    Spanish Sugar Cookies, 87

Strawberries with Chilled
   Zabaglione, 35 – 37
Sweet and Spicy Nut Brittle, 161
Three-Apple Crisp, 121
Tropical Fruits Foster, 51
Velvet Birthday Cake with Vanilla
   Buttercream Frosting, 133 – 35
Dips
   Deviled Crab Dip, 155
   Honest and Good Onion Dip, 156
Doorstop, Gourd, 98
Drainer, Beach-Pebble, 62
Dried Apples and Pears, 105

E
Eggs
   Asparagus and Basil Frittata, 30
   Elegant Eggs, 14
   Tortilla a la Española, 81

F
Favors, Glittery Cellophane, 143
Fireplaces
   Fireplace Candlescape, 143
   Flower-Filled Fireplace, 58
Floats, Root Beer, 62
Flowers
   Crystallized Flowers, 14
   Flower-Filled Fireplace, 58
   Fresh Flower Votives, 20
   Hostess (and Host) Flowers, 148
   Hostess with the Blooming Mostess, 58
   Lavender Wands, 61
   May Day (or Any Day) Baskets, 17
   Rosewater Refresher, 61
   Seashell Arrangement, 57
   Spring Bulbs, 105
   Violet Terrarium, 20
Fresh Flower Votives, 20
Frittata, Asparagus and Basil, 30
Frosting, Vanilla Buttercream, 135
Fruit. See also individual fruits
   Blushing Sangria, 90
   Putting Up, 101
   Tropical Fruits Foster, 51

G
Glittery Cellophane Favors, 143
Gourd Doorstop, 98
Grapefruit
   peeling and sectioning, 175
   Pink Grapefruit Shortcake, 173 – 75

H
Ham, Serrano, and Cider Blue Cheese
   Crostini, 158
Honest and Good Onion Dip, 156
Hostess (and Host) Flowers, 148
Hostess with the Blooming Mostess, 58
Hot Toddy, 148

I
Ice cream
   Root Beer Floats, 62
   Tropical Fruits Foster, 51

L
Lamb
   Petit Cassoulet, 170 – 72
Lavender Wands, 61
Lemons
   Lemon and Orange Sorbets in
   Citrus Cups, 89
   Limoncello, 22
Letter, Scented Love, 140
Limeade, Blueberry, 62
Limoncello, 22

M
May Day (or Any Day) Baskets, 17
Menus
   Autumn Birthday Celebration, 123
   Charades and Chardonnay, 151
   Easy Asian Kitchen Party, 39
   Garden-Inspired Lunch, 25
   Paella Party, 77
   Red, White, and Blueberry Breakfast, 65
   Soup for Supper, 107
   Sunday Dinner, 165
   Midsummer's Eve Syllabub, 57
   Minestrone, Autumn, with
   Tiny Turkey Meatballs, 113 – 14

Moss Candlescape, 98
Muffins, Old-Fashioned Blueberry, with
   Streusel Topping, 71 – 72
Mushrooms
   Summer Salad with Sherry Vinaigrette, 80
   Wild Mushroom Topping for Crusty
   Bread, 112

N
Nectarine-Ginger Pancakes with
   World's Easiest Blueberry Sauce, 68
Nuts. See also individual nuts
   Sweet and Spicy Nut Brittle, 161
   toasting, 111

O
Oak Leaves, Copper Foil, 98
Old-Fashioned Blueberry Muffins with
   Streusel Topping, 71 – 72
Onion Dip, Honest and Good, 156
Oranges
   Lemon and Orange Sorbets in Citrus
   Cups, 89
   Pomanders, 140
   Summer Salad with Sherry Vinaigrette, 80

P
Paella a la Valenciana, 84 – 86
Pancakes, Nectarine-Ginger,
   with World's Easiest Blueberry Sauce, 68
Parsnip Soup Sips, Curried, 157
Pears
   Dried Apples and Pears, 105
   Winter Salad with Roquefort and Pears, 169
Pecans
   Autumn Salad with Persimmons and
   Pecans, 111
   toasting, 111
Persimmons
   Autumn Salad with Persimmons
   and Pecans, 111
   Persimmons and Quince, 102
Petit Cassoulet, 170 – 72
Photo Display Tray, 144

Pink Grapefruit Shortcake, 173–75
Place Mats, Tea Towel, 22
Planter Citrus Tree, 147
Pomanders, 140
Pork
    Petit Cassoulet, 170–72
Potatoes
    Cape Cod Clam Chowder, 116–17
    Chestnut Soup with Black
        Pepper Cream, 119–20
    Tortilla a la Española, 81
Potpie, Chicken, 129–31
Prosciutto, Cherry Tomato, and
    Arugula Salad, 29
Pumpkin Pageant, 97
Putting Up, 101

Q
Quince and Persimmons, 102

R
Refreshing Cucumber Salad, 46
Rhubarb Chutney, 19
Rice
    Coconut Rice, 47
    Paella a la Valenciana, 84–86
Roast Chicken with Asian Flavors, 44
Roasted Beets with Blue Cheese
    and Walnuts, 127
Root Beer Floats, 62
Rosewater Refresher, 61
Runner, Tea Towel, 22

S
Salads
    Autumn Salad with Persimmons
        and Pecans, 111
    Basque Bell Pepper and Tomato Salad, 83
    Cherry Tomato, Arugula, and Prosciutto
        Salad, 29
    Refreshing Cucumber Salad, 46
    Spinach Salad with Shallot Vinaigrette, 128
    Summer Salad with Sherry Vinaigrette, 80
    Winter Salad with Roquefort and Pears, 169

Salt and Pepper Cellars, Walnut, 102
Salt and Pepper Shrimp, 43
Sangria, Blushing, 90
Sauces
    Cinnamon Applesauce, 101
    World's Easiest Blueberry Sauce, 68
Sausage
    Blueberry Turkey Sausage Patties, 70
    Paella a la Valenciana, 84–86
    Petit Cassoulet, 170–72
    Smoky Green Beans, 48
Scented Love Letter, 140
Seashell Arrangement, 57
Serrano Ham and Cider Blue Cheese
    Crostini, 158
Sherry Vinaigrette, 80
Shortcake, Pink Grapefruit, 173–75
Shrimp
    Paella a la Valenciana, 84–86
    Salt and Pepper Shrimp, 43
Smoky Green Beans, 48
Sorbets, Lemon and Orange, in Citrus
    Cups, 89
Soups
    Autumn Minestrone with Tiny
        Turkey Meatballs, 113–14
    Cape Cod Clam Chowder, 116–17
    Chestnut Soup with Black Pepper Cream,
        119–20
    Curried Parsnip Soup Sips, 157
Spanish Sugar Cookies, 87
Spinach Salad with Shallot Vinaigrette, 128
Spring Bulbs, 105
Stars, Bejeweled, 143
Strawberries with Chilled Zabaglione, 35–37
Summer Salad with Sherry Vinaigrette, 80
Sweet and Spicy Nut Brittle, 161
Syllabub, Midsummer's Eve, 57

T
Tea
    Hot Toddy, 148
    Tea Towel Place Mats and Runner, 22
Terrarium, Violet, 20

Three-Apple Crisp, 121
Tomatoes
    Basque Bell Pepper and Tomato Salad, 83
    Cherry Tomato, Arugula, and Prosciutto
        Salad, 29
    Paella a la Valenciana, 84–86
Tortilla a la Española, 81
Trees
    Alternative Christmas Tree, 147
    Planter Citrus Tree, 147
    Tropical Fruits Foster, 51
Turkey
    Autumn Minestrone with Tiny Turkey
        Meatballs, 113–14
    Blueberry Turkey Sausage Patties, 70
Twine Candleholders, 144

V
Vanilla Buttercream Frosting, 135
Vegetables. See also individual vegetables
    Autumn Minestrone with Tiny Turkey
        Meatballs, 113–14
    Chicken Potpie, 129–31
Velvet Birthday Cake with Vanilla
    Buttercream Frosting, 133–35
Violet Terrarium, 20

W
Walnuts
    Roasted Beets with Blue Cheese and
        Walnuts, 127
    Walnut Salt and Pepper Cellars, 102
Wild Mushroom Topping for Crusty
    Bread, 112
Wine
    Blushing Sangria, 90
    Midsummer's Eve Syllabub, 57
Winter Salad with Roquefort and
    Pears, 169

Z
Zabaglione, Chilled, Strawberries with,
    35–37

TABLE OF EQUIVALENTS

The exact equivalents in the following tables
have been rounded for convenience.

LIQUID/DRY MEASURES

U.S.	Metric
¼ teaspoon	1.25 milliliters
½ teaspoon	2.5 milliliters
1 teaspoon	5 milliliters
1 tablespoon (3 teaspoons)	15 milliliters
1 fluid ounce (2 tablespoons)	30 milliliters
¼ cup	60 milliliters
⅓ cup	80 milliliters
½ cup	120 milliliters
1 cup	240 milliliters
1 pint (2 cups)	480 milliliters
1 quart (4 cups, 32 ounces)	960 milliliters
1 gallon (4 quarts)	3.84 liters
1 ounce (by weight)	28 grams
1 pound	454 grams
2.2 pounds	1 kilogram

LENGTH

U.S.	Metric
⅛ inch	3 millimeters
¼ inch	6 millimeters
½ inch	12 millimeters
1 inch	2.5 centimeters

OVEN TEMPERATURE

Fahrenheit	Celsius	Gas
250	120	½
275	140	1
300	150	2
325	160	3
350	180	4
375	190	5
400	200	6
425	220	7
450	230	8
475	240	9
500	260	10